WITHDRAWN

Prophecy Interpreted

ESSAYS IN OLD TESTAMENT INTERPRETATION

Prophecy Interpreted

by John P. Milton

Augsburg Publishing House

Minneapolis, Minnesota

To

*the more than twelve hundred graduates
of Luther Theological Seminary who have
made teaching a pleasure and a privilege*

PREFACE

Prophecy is a big and important part of the Biblical message. The word suggests to us first of all the writing prophets, from Isaiah to Malachi; but prophecy in the Old Testament is by no means limited to them. The prophetic message was preached orally by many men who did not write books. We know some of them by name: men like Samuel, Gad, Nathan, Elijah, Elisha, and Micaiah. We have good reason to believe that there were others who remain unknown to us. The prophetic influence can be seen in Israel's history; it can be seen also in history writing in Israel. In the Hebrew Canon the historical books from Joshua to Kings are called "The Former Prophets," warning against an oversimplified definition of prophecy which makes it equivalent with prediction.

The New Testament also refers in significant fashion to the prophetic word as found in the Old Testament. Jesus said that He came to fulfill rather than to abolish the law and the prophets. New Testament writers make frequent use of Old Testament prophecy in their message. It is not only the direct quotation of prophecy or the claimed fulfilment of some prophetic word that is significant. Just as significant is the way in which the language and thought of the prophets are appropriated and made a part of the Christian message. Even more significant is the basic premise of the New Testament that there is a total fulfilment of the old in the new. In this fulfilment prophecy is included.

But what is prophecy? How shall we read and interpret it? It has its difficulties for the modern reader; even as it did for the Ethiopian eunuch who, in answer to Philip's question as to whether he understood what he was reading, replied quite naturally, "How can I, unless some one guides me?" (Acts 8:30, 31). The evangelist Luke says of Jesus after His resurrection, "Then he opened their minds to understand the scriptures" (Luke 24:45). In the same way the twentieth century Christian needs to be guided by some clearly discernible evangelical principles of interpretation if he is to understand the relevance of the prophetic word for today.

The four essays in this book are united in their attempt to state and to illustrate what the author believes to be such fundamental evangelical principles of interpretation of Old Testament prophecy. Each essay is an attempt to apply these principles to a specific question that confronts the thoughtful Christian as he reads the Old Testament scriptures, and especially the prophets, today. What is the message of the prophets for an age of fear such as ours? What is the verdict of the prophets, when seen in the light of the totality of scripture, as to the claim that the Holy Land belongs to Israel still by divine right? How is prophecy linked with the historical situation, past, present, and future; what are its "time-dimensions"? Can it be said of the prophets as well as of the apostles that they preached "the whole counsel of God"? The essays are not arranged in logical sequence. If there be some overlapping or repetition it is accounted for by the attempt to apply the same basic principles to four separate and yet related areas of prophetic interpretation.

JOHN P. MILTON

CONTENTS

Prophecy in an Age of Fear

Israel's Biblical Basis for Claiming the Holy Land

Prophecy in an Age of Fear

Introduction

This *is* an age of fear.

There have been times of fear before, great fear, and widespread; but the words of Jesus in Luke 21:26, "men fainting with fear and with foreboding of what is coming on the world," seem to be uniquely relevant to the situation in the world today. This is the atomic age. It is also an age of sharply clashing ideologies. It is an age of rising international tensions and of revolutionary technological, political, and social change. Men have gained a knowledge of cosmic forces for good or evil, but they have not learned the moral mastery of themselves under the law of love which can guarantee a right use of this knowledge. That is what makes our age in a unique sense an age of fear. We may paraphrase the words of the prophet Amos to fit this twentieth century,

> *Shall nuclear blasts be fired in the world,*
> *and the people not be afraid?* (Amos 3:6)

Since this is an age of fear it is not strange that there should be an increased interest in prophecy. We might call it an interest in eschatology, which has been defined as the

1

doctrine of the last or final things. At the heart of it is the very natural curiosity to know what lies ahead. In times of anxiety and distress it may become a cry of fear, "What will the end of these things be?" It expresses the hope for some assurance, perhaps in the form of some sure word of God, to calm fear. It has always been that way in times of great distress and danger. It is so today. It is not something that is found only in Christian circles, but neither is the Christian immune to this fear-motivated concern as to what the future may bring. There is in every age of fear a renewed interest in prophecy which gives evidence of this Christian concern for the future of the world. There is nothing strange nor wrong in that; it is a concern that is both natural and legitimate.

But all too often the emphasis in the study of prophecy is such as to increase rather than to allay fear. There are preachers and students of prophecy who seem to delight in playing on the fears and anxieties of people. They magnify the threat to peace and say little of "the things that make for peace." They are much concerned to identify men and nations and events today in terms of some specific Biblical prophecy. They focus attention on "antichrists" rather than on Christ; and they seem more concerned to prove what prophecy says about Russia, or about Israel, than to proclaim what it says about the kingdom of God. This emphasis may lead in its extreme form to "an end of the world" hysteria and presume to predict "times and seasons," which "the Father has fixed by his own authority" (Acts 1:7); but even in its more moderate form it does little to alleviate human fears in the face of threatening catastrophe. A wrong use of prophecy can never give to the human heart the faith and the hope and the love that casts out fear.

There is in this wrong use of prophecy a mistaken emphasis and a faulty exegesis. The emphasis is wrong because attention is focused primarily on transient events instead of on the redemptive activity of the living God. The exegesis is wrong because it does not understand the fundamental nature and purpose of prophecy, and therefore ignores basic evangelical principles of interpretation.

Let us try to state and to illustrate some of these fundamental principles of interpretation of Old Testament prophecy. Then in conclusion we shall return to the theme of "prophecy in an age of fear."

I. Historical Contemporaneity

The first significance of prophecy is as a message for the prophet's own day.

Three things are involved in this statement of interpretative principle:

1. The function of the prophet was first of all that of a preacher and teacher of the will of God. This does not rule out the element of prediction. It simply puts the primary emphasis where it belongs: on the prophetic message of repentance, and faith, and obedience; on the preaching concerning God and man and the covenant relationship between them; on the teaching concerning sin, and judgment, and salvation.

2. The message of the prophet reflects and reveals something of the historical situation to which it is directed. It clothes itself, as Ed. Riehm has so well said, in "local color" or "times-coloring."[1] It is effective preaching because it speaks to a definite life situation and is worded in terms of that situation. It may have a significance that goes far beyond the immediate situation; but our first task in interpretation is to

---

[1] Edward Riehm, *Messianic Prophecy*, tr. from German, 2nd ed., 1891, p. 133. Rev. ed., 1900, has "This historical dye."

ascertain what it meant for the faith and hope and religious life of those who lived within that historical situation, and to whom the prophet was sent as a spokesman of God.

3. Even the predictive element must be interpreted from within this framework of a religious message relevant for the day and the situation. What was the historical horizon for the prophet's vision? It may be that his prediction has been fulfilled. Unless it involves what Hebert has called "a clear continuity of theological principle" we have no right to project it beyond the situation visualized by the prophet himself.[2] Under no circumstances have we the right to treat Old Testament prophecies as disjointed parts of an eschatological picture puzzle to be assembled later without regard to historical origin.

A few illustrations:

Samuel was a prophet of the Lord just before and after the establishment of the monarchy in Israel. We have a summary of his prophetic message in I Samuel 12:19-25 and 15:22-23. The context makes it clear that he spoke God's word to king and people in the concrete historical situation of that day. He himself gives the key to his ministry in these words: "I will instruct you in the good and the right way" (12:23). There are familiar prophetic emphases in that instruction: fear the Lord, serve the Lord with all your heart, do not turn aside from following the Lord, do not turn aside after vain things which cannot profit or save; to obey is better than sacrifice. There is the reminder of what God has done for them in making them His people, and the assurance that He will not reject them if they serve Him faithfully; but there is also the warning, which may be called a conditional prediction, that "if you still do wickedly, you shall be swept away,

---

[2]A. G. Hebert, *The Throne of David*, 1946, pp. 130-131.

both you and your king." The prediction becomes unconditional in the case of Saul:

> *Because you have rejected the word of the Lord,*
> *he has also rejected you from being king.* (15:23)

We find the same kind of preaching in the books of the 8th century prophets, Amos, Hosea, Isaiah, and Micah. There is greater emphasis on sin and judgment, but the same evidence of historical contemporaneity. The message is to the people of Israel and Judah in the latter half of the 8th century B.C. The sin indicted is actual in that situation, the judgment predicted is imminent. The existing human situation is put under the judgment of God. That judgment concerns especially Israel, who was called to be the people of God but who, because of sins and transgressions against the covenant, is confronted with a new Egyptian bondage, a Babylonian captivity. There is a hope aspect which projects beyond the judgment and therefore involves predictive prophecy in a larger sense; but it too must be interpreted from within this historical milieu of which it was a part. A good example is the prophecy in Isaiah 9:1-7, which should be read against the background and within the setting of the Assyrian invasion in chapter 8. The adversative "but" rightly emphasizes the contrast between what is and what shall be, so that each must be understood in the context of the other.

Historical contemporaneity is more evident in some prophets than in others. It is very evident in the book of Jeremiah and in the first half of the book of Ezekiel. Here the prophecy is inextricably intertwined with the events leading up to and culminating in the Chaldean conquest, the fall of Jerusalem in 587-586 B.C., and the beginning of the Babylonian Captivity. In the same way the Assyrian background for the 8th century prophets is unmistakable. Historical contemporaneity is also evident in Nahum and Habakkuk. The book of Nahum is a prophecy of the downfall of Nineveh, which took place in 612 B.C. The theology of the book which motivates the prediction is timeless, and therefore just as relevant now as it was then; but the prediction itself belongs to a specific historical situation in the past. In Habakkuk we see the prophet wrestling with a faith-problem arising out of the conquests of the Chaldeans, "guilty men, whose own might is their god!" (1:11) Even where the eschatological aspect of some prophecies borders on apocalyptic, as in the book of Joel and in some sections of Ezekiel, it is not sound exegesis to assume that the element of historical contemporaneity is lacking just because it is difficult to identify the situation with certainty. We must begin our interpretation always with the working hypothesis that the first significance of a prophecy is as a message for the prophet's own day.

II. Covenant Background

A second fundamental principle of interpretation of Old Testament prophecy is this: Every prophecy must be interpreted in relation to the covenant of God with men.

Three things are involved also in this statement of interpretative principle:

1. The covenant is a major theological idea in Biblical religion. How significant it is can be seen only by the thoughtful Bible student who makes a serious study of it. Theologians like Karl Barth and Edmond Jacob have said that even the idea of creation is secondary to that of covenant in the Old Testament.[3] For the covenant has to do with God's redemptive activity in history; and the many facets of the divine covenant as seen in the Old Testament are bound together in the unity

---

[3] Edmond Jacob, *Theology of the Old Testament*, 1958, p. 136. See quotation from Barth, *Dogmatik III*, p. 106.

of His saving love. The so-called "covenants," with Noah, with Abraham, with Israel, with David, are essentially one covenant; and this covenant relationship is the framework for the Israelite understanding both of theology and of history.

2. The relation between covenant and history is especially significant to the Old Testament faith and to the prophetic message. The covenant not only presupposes that God is active in human history, but also that there is a purpose with and a goal to His activity. What that purpose is we learn from what God has said and done in the past. From a study of the covenant of blessing with Abraham, which in fulfilment became first the covenant with Israel and then the new covenant in the blood of Jesus Christ which is universal in scope, we can see that God's purpose from the beginning was a redemptive one, and that it is operative both in judgment and in salvation. All history must be seen in the light of this original covenant of God which reveals the fundamental outlines of His good and gracious, yet also holy and righteous, will for men.

3. It can readily be seen that there is a fundamental relationship also between covenant and prophecy. A right understanding of the covenant will help us in rightly interpreting prophecy, for every prophecy must be seen within the setting of the covenant promise and hope: it should be studied against the background of the covenant of blessing with Abraham, which through Moses became the national covenant with God's people Israel and through Jesus Christ found fulfilment in a universal covenant. If we see nothing more in the covenant with Abraham and with Israel than the promise of a seed and a land and material blessing, if we fail to see the spiritual vocation both of Abraham and of his seed to be a blessing to all mankind, we shall not understand the predominantly spiritual nature of the message of

the prophets either. The prophets were concerned with more than a nation and a land. They were concerned with spiritual things. They were not religious innovators. They believed in the covenant which God had made with their fathers, and they interpreted the present as well as the future in the light of this covenant from the past. But their understanding of the true nature of the covenant, and their interpretation of the situation that confronted them, was primarily religious rather than political.

A few illustrations:

When the prophet Hosea characterizes the sinfulness of his people as harlotry he does so because he wishes to portray in vivid imagery their unfaithfulness to the God of covenant love. Israel has been unfaithful to God even as the prophet's own wife had been unfaithful to him. In each instance it was a breach of covenant, the human marriage covenant being a symbol of the covenant between God and His people. The symbolic name of Lo-ammi is explained in language borrowed from the covenant relationship: "for you are not my people and I am not your God" (1:9). By their sin they have broken the covenant and have no right to call themselves the people of God. It is with this situation that the message of the prophet is concerned. What was God's word for Israel in such a situation as this? We shall not understand it unless we keep clearly in mind that the covenant implies a relationship between God and His people which involves both privilege and responsibility for the covenanted people. We shall not understand it unless we are equally clear as to the character and will of the covenant God. Hosea together with the rest of the prophets may deepen our understanding along both of these lines, but their message is not new except in its application to a new historical situation. The fundamentals of the covenant belong to God's activity and revelation in the past. Historical allusions abound in the book of Hosea, which are reminiscent of God's election of His people Israel and of His covenant with them and of the Exodus redemption which gave them, as it were, a new birth and a servant vocation.

> *When Israel was a child, I loved him,*
> *and out of Egypt I called my son.* (11:1)

When the prophet Isaiah indicts the sin of Israel as the rebellion of sons against a father he too uses an image which sets forth with dramatic vividness the offence against the God of covenant love. (1:2, 3).

It is against the background of the covenant, with its double aspect of spiritual privilege and responsibility, that we must understand the words of Amos,

> *You only have I known*
> *of all the families of the earth;*
> *therefore I will punish you*
> *for all your iniquities.* (3:2)

It is within the framework of the covenant that we must understand the requirements of God enunciated so simply and so strikingly by Micah,

> *He has showed you, O man, what is good;*
> *and what does the Lord require of you*
> *but to do justice, and to love kindness,*
> *and to walk humbly with your God?* (6:8)

It is the covenant from the past which enables us to grasp the significance of Jeremiah's prediction of a new covenant, similar to and yet far transcending the old. (31:31-34)

These are only a few selected illustrations; but the fact is that the whole prophetic message, whether it concern sin, judgment, or salvation, faith, hope, or love, religion, ethics, or history, past, present, or future, is inseparable from the basic faith of Israel in a God of covenant. Every prophecy must be interpreted in relation to this covenant of God with men.

III. Eschatological Significance

Because the covenant presupposes a divine activity in history which looks forward to a goal, there is a forward-looking or eschatological aspect also to all prophecy.

Several things are involved in this statement of interpretative principle:

1. It is to the divine purpose revealed in the covenant that the predictive aspect of prophecy attaches itself. Prediction must not be divorced from the covenant activity and purpose of God. The prophets were not predictive sharpshooters, who sought merely to satisfy human curiosity with respect to the future. They were preachers, who sought to renew faith in the ultimate fulfilment of the promises stated and implied in the very making of the covenant with Abraham and with Israel. Their hope for the future, which often became definite prediction, cannot be separated from their confidence in the God of the covenant who is faithful. That is why the present, the historically contemporaneous situation, is always seen both in the light of the past, or of the covenant with the fathers, and of the future, or of "the period of the great Restoration" (Acts 3:21, Moffatt).[4]

2. Since predictive prophecy is rooted in the covenant it may be wider in scope than specific prediction. This is not a contradiction in terms. There is a distinction, for instance, between the Messianic hope and the Messianic promise expressed in the form of a definite prediction, but both look to the future. There is a difference between the enunciation of a divine principle of judgment, which may find repeated ex-

---

[4] James Moffatt, *A New Translation of the Bible,* 1950.

pression in history, and the prediction of a specific judgment in time; yet both are forward-looking, and both belong to prophecy. The very faith in a God of covenant who is actively engaged in judgment and redemption, and who can always be counted on to act "in character," reacting in similar situations in the same divine way, is predictive. The theology of the prophets is pregnant with what may be called "the future hope."

3. The specific predictions may be classified in a twofold way. They may be predictions of events which are quite near, even imminent. In that case they are usually predictions of judgment, and they are the application of the spirit of the eternal covenant to the existing situation: sin brings chastisement; the holy community envisioned by the covenant must be achieved, if need be, by judgment. They may be predictions of events which are still in the remote, even indefinite, future. Then they are usually predictions of hope, and they represent the new prophetic insight which progressively deepens the understanding of the covenant itself and clarifies the nature of its final consummation. Biblical eschatology cannot be divorced from the covenant nor the Biblical covenant from eschatology: the one illumines the other.

4. It is equally true that we cannot divorce predictive prophecy from historical contemporaneity. No Old Testament prophecy completely rids itself of the local "times-coloring" of which we have spoken. Even the prophecies which come closest to speaking "New Testament language" give some evidence of their "Old Testament origin." But the "times-coloring" does not belong to the essence of a prophecy: it is rather the historical form in which the abiding truth of the prophecy is temporarily clothed. A prophecy may be much more spiritual and far more universal than a literal interpretation of this "times-coloring" would indicate. We may compare

a prophecy to a grain of wheat. Who would equate the wheat kernel with the husk? At a certain stage in the formation and growth of the wheat the husk is essential to the kernel which it clothes; but the husk exists only for the sake of the wheat. So it is with the "times-coloring" of prophecy.

A few illustrations:

The covenant with Abraham and with Israel centered around the threefold promise of a seed, a land, and a blessing. Each of the three had a significant place in the historically contemporaneous preaching of the prophets. Each one also had a significant eschatological aspect which is reflected in predictive prophecy.

God promised Abraham a seed (Hebrew "zerá," a singular collective noun) that should be in number as the dust of the earth (Gen. 13:6) and as the stars of heaven (Gen. 15:5; 22:17) and as the sand on the seashore (Gen. 22:17). Both Old Testament history and prophecy point to a fulfilment of the promise in Israel, who is called "the offspring (or the seed) of Abraham" (Isa. 41:8). But as the seed of Abraham Israel had also the vocation and the function of being God's people (Exodus 3:7), and God's son (Exodus 4:22), and God's servant (Exodus 4:23; Isa. 41:8). If we analyze these ideas carefully we find that they all have a religious connotation which combines spiritual privilege with spiritual responsibility. Israel is the recipient of blessing in order to be a blessing. Each of the functions just mentioned is taken up as a fundamental element in predictive prophecy; each looks forward to a greater future fulfilment than any that is recorded in the Old Testament history. According to the "times-coloring" of the prophetic language the "seed" is still Israel; but a deepening insight into the spiritual nature and purpose of Israel's vocation begins to prepare the way for the New Testament claim to a fulfilment of the promise of a seed in Jesus Christ (Gal. 3:16) and in those who are Christ's (Gal. 3:29), or in men of faith like Abraham's (Gal. 3:7, 9). The same thing takes place with the covenant ideas of Israel as son and servant and people of God. Predictive prophecy points to "a new thing" in the sense of a consummation of the vocation of Israel in a more spiritual and universal covenant; but it never rids itself of the "times-coloring" of the narrower national aspect of the covenant with Israel. The kernel and the husk are still joined together.

God also promised Abraham and his seed a land (Gen. 12:7), the land of Canaan. This promise looms large in Israel's history on two different occasions: before the conquest of Canaan under Joshua, when the original promise was fulfilled, and before the return from the Babylonian Captivity, when Israel experienced the fulfilment of a renewed promise of the land. Possession of the land was significant for a season in the working out of God's covenant plan with and through Israel; but if the New Testament is allowed to interpret the Old, the earthly land belongs to the husk rather than to the kernel of prophecy, being received by faith as a pledge of "a better country, that is, a heavenly one" (Heb. 11:16). A careful study of Old Testament prophecy will reveal that something of this faith shines through the rather earthly "times-coloring" even before the coming of Him who makes all things new (Rev. 21:5).

There is a comparable development of the promise of blessing, which is the very heart of the covenant with Abraham and with Israel. We speak now of the blessing *through* as well as *upon* Abraham's seed. Predictive prophecy is rich with promises of the blessing of God upon His people in fulfilment of His covenant with them. What do these promises finally mean? The actual wording of the prophecy is so often in terms of the history of Israel. For example, in Isaiah 40-66 we reach the highest peak in Israel's religious faith and

Messianic expectation; and yet, so much of the prophecy is colored by the imminent return from the Babylonian Captivity. Unless we make allowance for this "times-coloring" with which the prophecy is clothed we shall not understand the New Testament claim to a fulfilment which far transcends the letter of the prophecy. For in its ultimate fulfilment the promise of blessing is seen to be universal and not national, and completely spiritual in nature, mediated by the Christ who is in a unique sense Abraham's seed. For the New Testament claim at this point read Acts 3:26; Galatians 3:9 and 3:14; and Ephesians 1:3.

The prophecy in Isaiah 9:1-7 has been mentioned before in connection with historical contemporaneity. The birth and mission of the child whose name is Wonderful is set forth in language which at the same time reflects the "times-coloring" of the Old Testament and anticipates the New Testament reference of the prophecy to the ministry of Jesus Christ. The child comes to be a deliverer, in fulfilment of God's covenant with Israel, and a ruler, in accordance with the covenant with David; but the "times-coloring" of the king sitting upon the throne of David becomes the prophetic picture of Him who said, "My kingship (or my kingdom) is not of this world" (John 18:36).

The prediction of Amos, "that they may possess the remnant of Edom and all the nations who are called by my name" (Amos 9:12), implies the conquest of Edom and other Gentile nations and their incorporation by force into the national Israel; which could be one way of sharing the blessing of the covenant, at the same time as it indicated the victory of God and of His people over their enemies. The imagery fits the historically contemporaneous situation. But there are other Old Testament prophecies, such as in Isaiah 2 and Micah 4, which have already dropped the imagery of physical conquest in favor of the more spiritual one of a voluntary seeking of the Lord in response to invitation, and have thus prepared the way for the New Testament use of the Amos passage in Acts 15:17, "that the rest of men may seek the Lord, and all the Gentiles who are called by my name." In saying this we are not unaware that there is a problem of textual criticism also involved in James' quotation of Amos at the Jerusalem conference.

The prophecy in Jeremiah 31:31-34 is an even clearer illustration of what we mean by the attachment of predictive prophecy to previous covenant and by the eschatological significance of the covenant. Every item in the new covenant of Jeremiah is in some way anticipated in the covenant with Abraham and with Israel at Sinai. In one sense it is simply a reaffirmation of what God has been trying to do all along. It is in the prediction of the final realization of this objective that it so far transcends the old as to deserve to be called new. The prophecy still leaves unsaid that this can be brought to pass only through the coming of a Saviour like Jesus Christ. It does illustrate the principle that there is a forward-looking or eschatological aspect to prophecy which both reflects and illumines the divine purpose revealed in the covenant.

IV. The Shortened Perspective

Every prophecy must be interpreted in the light of "the shortened perspective" which is characteristic of Biblical prophecy.

At least three things are involved in this statement of interpretive principle:

1. In the prophetic message the eschatological goal of the covenant is often seen as coming soon. It seems to be expected right after and in direct relation to the historical situation of the moment to which the message of the prophet is directed.

There is a sequence of purpose which may easily be confused with a calendar of times and seasons. The prophet is concerned about the present unfaithfulness of God's people, which contradicts the purpose of the covenant and makes the experience of a genuine covenant relationship impossible; and as the messenger of God he pronounces judgment, often in concrete historical terms, upon the present evil situation. Some students of prophecy have supposed that this was the only function of a true prophet. The classic definition of a true prophet is said to be the one given in Micah's description of himself,

> *But as for me, I am filled with power,*
>   *with the Spirit of the Lord,*
>   *and with justice and might,*
>   *to declare to Jacob his transgression*
>   *and to Israel his sin.* (3:8)

We may ask, however: *Why* does a prophet declare to his people their transgression and sin? Why does God raise up prophets to preach judgment at all? It is certainly not for the joy of denunciation nor for the purpose of destruction. As J. E. McFadyen has said, "The last word of God can never be destruction. —The living God would not be God, if His purpose were to be ultimately frustrated."[5] The prophets were men of faith in the living God, who is the faithful God of covenant promise; because they believed that God is faithful they hoped for a glorious experiential fulfilment of the covenant, and they declared this hope as if it were on the horizon just beyond the present judgment.

2. Because of this close sequence of purpose between past promises and present reality and future hope it is natural that they should phrase their hope not only in the language of the covenant but in the thought-forms of the historically con-

---

[5] J. E. McFadyen, *A Cry for Justice*, 1912, p. 136.

temporaneous situation. We turn again to Isaiah 9:1-7 for an especially striking illustration. There is a series of significant contrasts in vs. 1-5: between the present contempt and the future glory of the land of Zebulun and Naphtali; between the present darkness of the Assyrian conquest and the future light; between the distress and anguish of the present, as the nation is decimated almost to the point of destruction, and the future joy when it shall again be multiplied and blessed; between the present oppression by a foreign conqueror and the future deliverance "as on the day of Midian"; between the present experience of bloody, tumultuous war and the future experience of peace. The series culminates in the prediction of a Wonder-child of the house of David, and by Him the kingdom of David will be restored. It is a beautiful picture of the prophetic hope of restoration, through which shines the larger hope of covenant consummation. The "times-coloring," however, is still largely that of the national history of Israel. The hope of consummation of the promises of the covenant is beautifully relevant for every age; but the nature of the consummation in the spiritual ministry and reign of our Lord Jesus Christ still needs to be clarified. The clarification comes as God acts in history as His own interpreter.

3. It is significant that the prophets do not say much about "times and seasons" for the fulfilment of their hopes and predictions. There are exceptions, of course, such as the seventy years of the Babylonian Captivity in the book of Jeremiah; but a mathematical approach even to this prediction may miss the point of the prophet's message, which is religious rather than political. The prophetic phrase, "in the latter days," is a good example of the indeterminate nature of their time-references. When will "the latter days" begin? To the prophets they seem to mean the time of the ideal or Messianic future. They do not presume to say just when these days will begin.

The prophetic phrase points rather to a definite goal in the indefinite future. The emphasis is on the promised goal, not on the time when it will be reached. Out of their faith in the covenant purpose and goal of God they keep affirming, "He will do it!" They do not say when it will be. For the words of Jesus were true of them as they are of us, "It is not for you to know times or seasons which the Father has fixed by his own authority" (Acts 1:7).

A few illustrations:

The message of the book of Joel centers around a calamitous locust plague that has come upon the land and seems to the prophet to be the beginning of the very day of the Lord. Immediately after the description of the devastation by the locusts, and the prophetic pleading for a penitent return to the Lord, comes a picture of restoration (2:18ff.). The sequence of events is clear: 1) the removal of the northerner, or the locusts, and the restoration of material blessing and prosperity to the land (2:18-25); 2) the renewed presence of God with His people, which seems to imply permanence, and the renewal of a right attitude by His people towards Him (2:26-27); 3) the outpouring of God's Spirit on all flesh (2:28-29), which in the New Testament is related to the day of Pentecost (Acts 2); 4) the appearance of cosmic portents of the coming of the great and terrible day of the Lord (2:30-32), which seems to imply the final judgment; 5) the judgment on the nations in the valley of Jehoshaphat (3:1-15), which implies the victory of God over all who have been enemies of His people (the nations named all belong to ancient history, hence their relevance for today can only be in a representative capacity); and 6) the idyllic blessing and peace of God's people in Jerusalem, "for the Lord dwells in Zion" and will be "a refuge to his people" (3:16-21). The ideas in the prophecy are definite, but the time element is not: the near and the distant, and the constantly recurring events are all blended in one picture, after the manner of mountain peaks and ranges when seen from a distance. The sequence of purpose alone is clear.

The prophet who speaks in Isaiah 40-55 is a gospel preacher with a glorious message of exultant hope. In that message the very evident "times-coloring" is that of the imminent return from the Babylonian Captivity; and it may well be that the prophet expected the return to usher in "the great Restoration" (Acts 3:21). In this he was mistaken; but not as to the reality of the restoration itself to which the majestic spiritual overtones of his message bear witness. It is as if through the telescopic lens of the divine activity in relation to His covenant people and purpose *now* we are given to see with the prophet a glimpse also of the glorious promised finale. The prophecy does not tell us that a valley of five centuries of time lies between the "new thing" which God was about to do then in redeeming His people from Babylon and the greater "new creation" which was foreshadowed by the exalted imagery of the prophetic faith and hope, even the redemptive act of God in Christ. The shortened perspective of prophecy cautions us to pay more attention to what it reveals of fundamental religious faith than to what it may seem to say about the more exciting matter of the time when these things shall be.

V. *The Fulfilment Greater Than the Prediction*

It must be borne in mind in interpreting prophecy that the fulfilment is almost always greater than the prediction.

What is involved in this statement of interpretative principle?

1. It is wrong to assume that if we are to claim fulfilment of a prophecy there must be a literal correspondence between

the prediction and the fulfilment. This mistaken premise might lead to the conclusion that few if any genuine prophecies have been fulfilled. It would require a radical revision of the New Testament viewpoint as to the fulfilment of Old Testament prophecy. There is within each prophecy a central idea, and when this has been fulfilled we may claim fulfilment for the prophecy as a whole. We need not look for a literal fulfilment of all its details.

2. It is also wrong to assume that where there seems to be a literal correspondence between the prediction and the historical event which fulfils it this is the really important thing to stress in interpretation of the prophecy. The chief concern of prophecy is not to prove that God can predict events with meticulous exactness before they happen; nor to construct a calendar of events which with divine precision charts the course of history beforehand, so as to make unnecessary the walk by faith and not by sight. A prophecy may be a sign: but if so, the thing signified will be what we have called its central religious idea. We do not ignore the letter of prophecy in interpretation; but we do look beyond and beneath it for the essential truth that it is meant to express.

3. In saying that the fulfilment is greater than the prediction we mean that it is clearer, that it is more specific in reference, that it has a more definite spiritual emphasis. The old covenant becomes new. The kingly reign of Yahve over His people Israel becomes the universal and eternal reign of the King of kings and the Lord of lords. Israel as the people of God becomes the Church of Jesus Christ. The Old Testament "servant of the Lord" becomes the only beloved Son of God, who humbles himself to take on the form of a servant. The coming of God to redeem His people is seen in fulfilment as the coming of Jesus Christ to be the Redeemer

of the world. The covenant with the family of David leads at last to Him who said, "My kingship is not of this world." There *is* predictive prophecy in the Old Testament; but we need the commentary of redemptive history, or of the New Testament gospel, *to declare all that was really essential in the prophecy.* The relation between the Old Testament and the New is like that between the acorn and the oak: the oak is in the acorn, but the acorn must grow into an oak before we can know the true relationship between the two. If we stressed the letter of prophecy only we would never get beyond the acorn.

A few illustrations:

In the book of Micah the prophecy against Samaria (1:6-7) and the prophecy against Jerusalem (3:12) seem to be equally specific. The context of both indicates the Assyrian invasion in the eighth century B.C., when according to Isaiah Assyria was the rod of God's anger which He used for chastisement (Isa. 10:5ff.). Both of the Micah passages are predictions of a judgment which reduces the city to ruins. The first was literally fulfilled when Sargon of Assyria captured and destroyed Samaria in 722-721 B.C. The second was a "conditional" prophecy, as we see from Jeremiah 26:16-19, and the city of Jerusalem escaped. Later, in a new historical situation, it too was captured and destroyed, by Nebuchadnezzar of Babylon in 587 B.C.; but never as completely and permanently as Samaria. Yet, even in the 8th century, Jerusalem did not escape judgment, which is the central idea of the prophecy. See Isaiah 1:5-9 for a more exact picture of what actually happened. Which is the more significant in the Micah prophecy, the central idea of judgment, which was fulfilled, or the details of the prediction, which proved to be conditional?

In Isaiah 7:14 there are two significant words: the Hebrew "ha'almah," which means a young woman of marriageable

age, and the name Immanuel, which in translation means
"God with us." The central idea in the prophecy is the latter:
the child is to be the sign of God's presence with His people,
which ties in with the very heart of the covenant of blessing,
"I will be your God." God is ever faithful on His part to this
original covenant promise. He is ever ready to let His people
experience on their part that He is their God *if* they truly seek
Him in covenant faith and obedience. But every repetition
of the promise, including the Immanuel prophecy, foreshadowed an even more wonderful experience to come, when
God Himself would take on human flesh and dwell among
men. We say that the central idea of God's abiding presence
with His people *foreshadowed* the Incarnation. We can go
no further. The Immanuel prophecy is a glorious one, but
even here the fulfilment is greater than the prediction. So it
is also with the reference to the mother of the child as
"ha'almah." See the present author's pamphlet, "God's Word
to Men."[6]

We need scarcely mention Isaiah 9:1-7 again. The application of vs. 1-2 to the Galilean ministry of Jesus in Matthew
4:12-17 takes us far beyond the letter of the prophecy as
seen in the context of the Assyrian invasion; but the central
idea in the prophecy of covenant restoration and fulfilment
is certainly related to the ministry of Jesus. The New Testament does not err in saying that there was a fulfilment; but
the fulfilment is greater than the prediction, in the same sense
in which the new covenant is greater than the old.

The servant of the Lord in Isaiah 40-55 is first of all Israel.
The vocation and function of Israel was to serve the Lord
in a unique way by being a blessing to all the nations of the
earth. This is a part of the covenant background as well as
of the historical contemporaneity reflected in the prophecy;

---

[6]John P. Milton, *God's Word to Men,* 1953, pp. 8-11.

but in his "peak" chapter about the Suffering Servant, the prophet indicates that the servant function of Israel pointed beyond itself to One who should fulfil it in an altogether unique way, He who "was wounded for our transgressions" and "by whose stripes we are healed." The New Testament makes the final identification of the Servant with Jesus Christ. In so doing it implies that he is the fulfilment not only of the Servant prophecies but also of Israel's servant vocation. The fulfilment, however, includes the Christian Church, which in New Testament language is the body of Christ. The whole concept of Israel as the servant of God is predictive, but its ultimate significance is clarified only by the fulfilment. The fulfilment confirms that Israel's servant vocation, like yours and mine, had significance only in relation to Jesus Christ who fulfils it. The fulfilment is greater than the prediction.

VI. The Unifying Focal Point

All prophecy has one central focus, in respect to purpose, in religious emphasis, in its essential time-element, viz., God's redemptive purpose and activity in history which heads up in Christ.

From the viewpoint of Christian faith this is the most significant interpretative principle of all. It involves a number of things:

1. The first is the significance of the Incarnation of Jesus Christ as a dividing-line in the interpretation of Old Testament prophecy. That dividing-line is dramatized by our division of history into "b.c." and "a.d." The Incarnation is the dividing-line between the old and the new. In terms of Biblical interpretation it is the dividing-line between prophecy and fulfilment. We would include in the Incarnation, of course, the life and ministry of Christ that it introduced; and we

include also the vital relationship of the Church to Jesus Christ as His body, through which He still works in the world. If, as Christian faith asserts, the Incarnation is a fact of history, then it follows inexorably that all Old Testament teaching must be re-examined in its light and all interpretation of Old Testament prophecy must be related to this new event which has the effect of making all things new.

2. The second is the specific significance of the Incarnation for an understanding of Old Testament history. It puts that history very clearly and definitely into the place of the preliminary and the temporary, whose real meaning and purpose cannot be fully seen apart from its fulfilment in Christ. From the Biblical point of view there is nothing strange in speaking of a fulfilment of history. The covenant concept involves just this faith in a living God whose redemptive activity in history is an activity with a goal. The Incarnation, in the inclusive sense of all that belongs to the ministry or mission of Christ as the Son of God and the Saviour of the world, is that goal. The coming of Christ ushered in the new age; it was the beginning of "the latter days": it spelled "Fulfilment" with a capital F. However important in the plan of God may have been His people Israel, or His servants the prophets, or the religion, culture, and way of life of the Old Testament, they all with John the Baptist must say before the Christ, "He must increase, but I must decrease" (John. 3:30). The fulfilment of Israel's history is in and through Jesus Christ.

3. The third is the specific significance of the Incarnation for the understanding of Old Testament predictive prophecy. We have already said that some predictions belonged to the historically contemporaneous situation of the prophet and were fulfilled soon after they were spoken. We might have said that there are comparatively few direct predictions of

the coming of a personal Messiah. The future hope that looks for the day of "the great Restoration," or for the day of covenant fulfilment, or for the day of the redemption of God's afflicted people, or for the day when men shall really know the Lord, or for the day when God's kingdom shall have come in all its universal scope and eternal glory—this future hope is prominent and, because we believe it to be a hope wrought by the Spirit of God, prophetic. If, however, we would see the relation of all this to Christ in His Incarnation, we would be hindered rather than helped by a completely literal interpretation: an interpretation which does not distinguish between local "times-coloring" and basic religious ideas, which does not recognize that the Bible is the record of sacred rather than of political history, and which makes no allowance for the clearly evident progressiveness in revelation.

4. The fourth is the danger of misinterpretation of prophecy by removing texts from their historical context and referring them to some historically unrelated situation in the remote future, perhaps in the time of the end. If Christ be indeed the real goal and fulfilment of Israel's covenant hope and Messianic expectation, then in relation to Old Testament prophecy His person, His life, His mission, His teaching, is like the funnel in the hourglass: in order to be valid and relevant in the new age every prophecy must funnel through the illuminating and transforming reality of the Incarnation and of Pentecost. That is, it must have a continuing significance in relation to the person and work of Jesus Christ. That does not mean that only direct and exclusive predictions of the Messiah are genuine and valid prophecy. It does mean that prophecy is significant only in relation to God's plan of salvation through Jesus Christ. The enmity of and the judgment upon the nations, for example, has no religious relevance apart from its relation to the kingdom of God. The nations

on whom the prophets pronounced judgment were nations who *in their own day* had shown hostility *to Israel as the people of God.* Israel as a political entity is not the significant thing in prophecy: the focus is on Israel as a religious community, which God has chosen to call "my people." As such Israel is representative of the people of God in the new age, even as her ancient enemies are representatives of the enemies of God and His kingdom in the new age. In the sense of "a clear continuity of theological principle," the old prophecies may be surprisingly relevant for our day. It is when we look for direct and literal predictions concerning nations and individuals and events in the twentieth century that we violate a fundamental principle of prophecy.

A few illustrations:

Throughout the Old Testament it is Israel that is called and separated to be the people of God. It was to Israel that God said, "You shall be my own possession (Moffatt, 'my own prized possession';[7] AJV, 'Mine own treasure'[8]) among all peoples—and a holy nation" (Exod. 19:5, 6). The sign of their separation as a holy nation unto the Lord was circumcision (Gen. 17). The purpose of their separation was to serve the Lord in a missionary vocation: as the seed of Abraham they were to *be* a blessing as well as to inherit a blessing. Their election was sealed by a "berith 'olam," or an everlasting covenant. It is to this people and of this people as the people of God that the prophets speak. They speak, as we have said before, in language that is colored throughout by the election experience and the covenant status of Israel. Now and then a little glimpse is given of the place of the Gentiles in relation to this favored position of Israel, as if they could hope to become proselytes to Israel's faith; but the prophetic per-

---

[7] James Moffatt, *A New Translation of the Bible,* 1950.
[8] *American Jewish Version,* a new translation of the Holy Scriptures, 1917.

spective is essentially that of the future history, the hopes and fears, the covenant expectation, of Israel. Even the new covenant of Jeremiah is worded as if it were to be a new covenant with Israel. The prophets do stress increasingly the fundamental spiritual nature of the covenant: instead of the circumcision of the flesh they emphasize the circumcision of the heart (see especially Jeremiah); they insist on the need of a new heart and a new spirit (Ezekiel); they predict the outpouring of the Spirit of God upon all flesh (Joel); they present a picture of the Servant of the Lord which is completely spiritual in its significance (Isaiah 53); but nevertheless each prophecy seems directed to God's Old Testament people, Israel. Then Christ comes; and with His coming all these things that are said of Israel are transferred to the New Testament people of God, the believers in Jesus Christ, all those who are men of faith like Abraham, the Church of Christ within which all distinctions and divisions cease. "There is neither Jew nor Greek, there is neither slave nor free, there is neither male nor female; for you are all one in Christ Jesus. And if you are Christ's, then you are Abraham's offspring, heirs according to promise." (Gal. 3:28, 29) Ideally, this is the goal of Old Testament history and of Old Testament prophecy. We readily admit that the ideal has not yet become complete reality in the experience of mankind; but it is the character of the new age, and in its light Christian faith and Christian hope interprets prophecy.

In the light of this development it is easy to see how Isaiah 40-55 can be at the same time a prophecy of the return of the Jews from the Babylonian Captivity and of the redeeming work of Jesus Christ. The full realization of Israel's hopes did not come with the return from Babylon; and yet, their hopes were not false. The return under Zerubbabel was a step on the way toward the final fulfilment, of which it was itself a type and a prophecy. For just as in the election of Israel

God had in view the blessing of all nations, so in the redemption of Israel from captivity He had in view the redemption of humanity from sin and death; and through the eyes of the prophets we see a picture of redemption that encompasses both. The many fragments of prophecy (Weymouth, Hebrews 1:1),[9] the recurring central ideas of Israel's faith and hope, are seen in the clarifying unity of fulfilment in the gospel of the Son of God. For He is the focus (Swedish "brännpunkten") of all Biblical prophecy.

VII. *The Double Emphasis in Prophecy*

Our interpretation of prophecy must be guided by a clear recognition of the two chief points of emphasis in Old Testament prophecy: judgment and redemption.

Two things are involved in this statement of interpretative principle: the goal of God's covenant and the way to that goal.

1. We have said that the covenant of God in Old Testament history and theology envisions a goal. We have said that God who acts in history does so not aimlessly but with purpose to reach the covenant goal. We have not thus far defined that goal except to call it the consummation of the covenant and "the period of the great Restoration." We have emphasized that Jesus Christ, if we think of Him in the comprehensiveness of His mission, is the goal of prophecy; but just what does this mean in the way of experience and future events for humanity?

There are many facets to the Biblical answer to this question. It is easier to describe some of these facets than it is to define the whole. We shall try this method of picturing the goal as the Bible indicates it.

---

[9] Richard Francis Weymouth, *The New Testament in Modern Speech,* 4th ed., 1924.

There is a goal indicated in the very covenant of blessing with Abraham, "in you all the families of the earth will be blessed" (Gen. 12:3, RSV mg.).[10] Ever since the creation and the fall of man it has been God's active desire to bless all men "in Christ with every spiritual blessing" (Eph. 1:3). Genesis 12:3 and Ephesians 1:3 are like the two ends of a string: in one we see the prophetic beginning, in the other the gospel fulfilment. Read Eph. 1:3-14 with this thought in mind and see if you do not agree that here is fulfilment of both Biblical history and prophecy: every spiritual blessing, the status of a holy people, sonship with God, the experience of God's glorious grace and love, redemption, forgiveness, inheritance, a creation united in praise of the glory of Jesus Christ. Is anything essential omitted?

There is a goal indicated in the prophecy of Jeremiah concerning the new covenant which God will make (31:31-34). If we look through the "times-coloring" of the prophecy to the New Testament interpretation we see a consummation of the old in the new: a spiritually responsive people at last; the Torah or law of God finally written upon their hearts, as a guide into the good and gracious will of God; a realization at last of the perfect fellowship between God and men envisioned by the covenant words "their God" and "my people"; a universal knowledge of God, in the deep inner and experiential sense which the prophets always had in mind when they spoke of "knowing the Lord"; a complete and permanent experience of the forgiveness of sin, that sin which had stood hindering in the way of true covenant fellowship with God. A glorious picture; and yet, a comparison with Ephesians 1 quickly reveals how much more explicit is the gospel than the prophecy. It also reveals, however, how much they have in common, pointing in their different ways to the same goal.

---

[10] *The Revised Standard Version* of the Holy Bible, 1952.

There is a goal indicated in Isaiah 40-66. Bracker summarizes it for us in his fine outline of these chapters in "Der Knecht Jehova."[11]

A. chs. 40-48 Cyrus, or the redemption of the Jews from Babylon, as a prophetic shadow (or silhouette) of the redemption of humanity from sin.

B. chs. 49-57 Christ, or the redemption of humanity from sin through the Servant of the Lord.

C. chs. 58-66 The new world, or the redemption of the world from "Vergänglichkeit" (i.e., from that which is transitory and passing away) as a result of the redemption from sin.

The prophecy culminates in the sweeping declaration,

> For behold, I create new heavens
> and a new earth;
> and the former things shall not be remembered
> or come into mind. (65:17)

The New Testament simply adds, *"in which righteousness dwells"* (II Peter 3:13)

There is a goal indicated in Revelation 21:3, 4: "Behold the dwelling of God is with men. He will dwell with them, and they shall be his people, and God himself will be with them; he will wipe away every tear from their eyes, and death shall be no more, neither shall there be mourning nor crying nor pain any more, for the former things have passed away." The fundamental covenant idea of the gracious presence of God with His people gives rise to the hope of victory over death and of eternal joy.

The goal that is set before us in both the Old Testament and the New is pictured in bright and variegated colors; but it is always the goal of hope for the fulfilment of God's cove-

---

[11] D. Bracker, *Der Knecht Jehova*, 1924 (Vol. 3 of Jesaja, der Seher). Tr. of inhaltsverzeichnis, or Table of Contents.

nant promises. In one form or another this is the closing note
of almost every prophetic book in the Old Testament. "The
kingdom shall be the Lord's" (Obadiah 21). "For the Lord
dwells in Zion" (Joel 3:21). "I will restore the fortunes of my
people Israel" (Amos 9:14). "Thou wilt show faithfulness to
Jacob and steadfast love to Abraham, as thou hast sworn to
our fathers from the days of old" (Micah 7:20). "I will joy
in the God of my salvation" (Habakkuk 3:18). "The Lord
your God is in your midst—he will renew you in his love"
(Zephaniah 3:17). "From this day on I will bless you" (Haggai
2:19). "And the name of the city henceforth shall be, The
LORD is there" (Ezekiel 48:35). "And on that day there
shall be inscribed on the bells of the horses, 'Holy to the
LORD.' And the pots in the house of the Lord shall be as
the bowls before the altar; and every pot in Jerusalem and
Judah shall be sacred to the Lord of hosts" (Zechariah
14:20-21).

> *For as the new heaven and the new earth*
> *which I will make*
> *shall remain before me, says the Lord;*
> *so shall your descendants and your name remain.*
> *From new moon to new moon,*
> *and from sabbath to sabbath,*
> *all flesh shall come to worship before me,*
> *says the Lord.* (Isaiah 66:22-23)

The composite picture given by such passages as these is that
of the victory of God and His kingdom over every foe, of
unbroken fellowship between a people holy to the Lord and
their everpresent faithful God, of a new covenant which does
not supplant but fulfils the old. It is in a setting such as this
that we must read the words of Jesus in Matthew 5:17,
"Think not that I have come to abolish the law and the
prophets; I have come not to abolish them but to fulfil them."

Such is the goal of history that is indicated by prophecy.

How then does the God who according to prophecy acts in history move towards the fulfilment of this goal?

2. He does so in two ways. The two are so closely related that one often seems to be the reverse side of the other. There is nevertheless a distinction between the two that needs to be kept in mind. We speak now of judgment and of redemption. These are the two motifs that run through all of Biblical prophecy as well as history.

Judgment

God moves forward towards the goal of His covenant with men by judgments.

Much of prophecy is devoted to the preaching or declaration of judgment. John D. Davis defines the function of prophecy well when he says, "The law presents the commandments and claims of Jehovah to man; prophecy passes judgment on conduct in the light of God's revealed will and explains the object of God's dealings with men."[12] The conduct on which this judgment is passed is in the first instance that of Israel as the covenant nation, the people of God. Naturally the judgment applies to the individual Israelite as well; and in view of the representative character of Israel it applies to the people of God also in the New Testament dispensation. It applies to the nations who in their conduct show themselves to be enemies of Israel and of Israel's God; but it is first of all within the covenant relationship that prophecy passes this judgment on conduct in the light of the Torah or law of God. For what A. B. Davidson says of the law is equally true of prophecy: it was "given to the people in covenant."[13]

---

[12] John D. Davis, *A Dictionary of the Bible*, 4th ed., 1924, Art. "Wisdom."
[13] A. B. Davidson, *The Theology of the Old Testament*, 1905, p. 280.

The reason for the prophetic preaching of judgment is the presence of sin. We may be more specific still and say that it is the sin of unfaithfulness to the covenant; for it is in this basic sin of faithlessness that the prophets see the root of every sin. Israel's conduct as God's people did not harmonize with the covenant ideal. Called to be a holy nation, holy to the LORD, and devoted to Him in humble faith and whole-hearted obedience, they had turned "every one to his own way" (Isaiah 53:6). With such an attitude on their part there could be no true covenant fellowship, however faithful God might be on His part. With such an attitude they could not fulfil their mission of being a kingdom of priests and a holy nation, through whom God would bless all the nations of the earth. We might say that God, who cannot condone sin in the conduct of His people nor fail to react when they forget Him (Hosea 2:13), faced two alternatives: either He could wash His hands of them, as He once proposed to Moses that He would do (Exodus 32:9-10); or He could seek to bring about reformation through the preaching of judgment unto repentance. The message of the prophets is proof to us that God chose the latter way. We find a clear statement of this one aspect of the prophetic function in the great verse in Micah 3:8,

> *But as for me, I am filled with power,*
> *with the Spirit of the Lord,*
> *and with justice and might,*
> *to declare to Jacob his transgression*
> *and to Israel his sin.*

The primary purpose of the prophetic preaching of judgment was repentance; but often there was no repentance. The preaching seemed to be in vain. But God is not one to be mocked: He is not only a God who speaks to men by the mouth of prophets whom He sends, He is also a God who acts, so that the very events of history are made to speak His will.

Hence the prophetic preaching takes on the concrete form of prediction of what the God who acts will do when His people refuse to hear and so despise His word to them. His judgments take on the external form of a national experience of calamity, of conquest, of captivity: the Assyrian captivity in the latter part of the eighth century B.C., the Babylonian captivity in the sixth century. Judgment must begin at the house of God; for the divine purpose with the judgment is chastisement rather than destruction, and the divine goal is still a penitent people that will truly seek the Lord. It is only when men or nations persist in their enmity or in their indifference to the living God and to His gracious covenant will, that the judgment becomes destruction, and the declaration of judgment a declaration of the victory of God over all who oppose His holy will and His kingly power.

We have spoken of the judgment *motif* in Scripture, as if it were an oft-repeated rather than a once-for-all experience. It is a good illustration of that "clear continuity of theological principle" of which Hebert speaks.[14] God acts in judgment wherever judgment is called for by the situation which confronts. He acts in judgment because He is holy, but also because it is a means to an end. Without it there can never be a holy nation such as was envisioned from the beginning of the covenant with Israel (see Exodus 19:5-6, and also the New Testament application in I Peter 2:9-10). Without it there can not be the hope of new heavens and a new earth in which righteousness dwells (II Peter 3:13). There is a chastening aspect to God's judgments which is fully as significant as the punitive, as long as it is still the day of grace and salvation for mankind. Nevertheless the punitive aspect is also there; and with each experience of it in man's history on this earth

---

[14] A. G. Hebert, *The Throne of David*, 1946, pp. 130-131.

there is a prophetic reminder that God is not mocked, that His kingdom will come, that the final victory in the conflict between good and evil will be His: each judgment act becomes as it were a peak in a mountain range that rises ever higher and higher, until it seems to point forward to a greater and a final judgment to come. Of that final judgment the Old Testament seldom if ever speaks in direct terms; but it is foreshadowed by the judgments in time. It is the prophetic phrase "the day of the Lord" that in a special way embodies this judgment motif, wherein the judgment is seen as near, as repeated, as having a covenant-related purpose, as having also a final eschatological quality and effect.

Redemption

Parallel to and projecting beyond the motif of judgment is that of redemption.

God moves forward towards the goal of His covenant with men by redemptive acts, or acts of deliverance.

From one point of view, of course, redemption may be regarded as the very goal of history; but from the prophetic viewpoint it is also a divine activity that is always present *in* history, and which leads to the goal. The greatest of the redemptive experiences in the Old Testament narrative is that of the Exodus. Another almost as significant is that of the return from the Babylonian Captivity. These have a special importance both in relation to Biblical prophecy and to Biblical history because they concern the whole covenant people of God, and there is in each case a representative character to the event. Israel in the Old Testament represents God's people down through the ages. For just as Hosea, speaking as a prophet of God, addresses Israel in the day of "the great Restoration,"

> " . . . *And I will have pity on Not pitied,*
>   *and I will say to Not my people,*
>   *'You are my people';*
>   *and he shall say, 'Thou art my God' "* (2:23),

so Peter, speaking as an apostle of Jesus Christ, says to them
who have been ransomed from sin and death "with the
precious blood of Christ":

"But you are a chosen race, a royal priesthood, a holy nation,
God's own people, that you may declare the wonderful deeds
of him who called you out of darkness into his marvelous
light. Once you were no people but now you are God's people;
once you had not received mercy but now you have received
mercy" (I Peter 2:9-10).

The external redemptive experience of Israel, which certainly had profound religious implications, is a type of the
fundamentally spiritual redemption which is in and through
Jesus Christ. There *is* prophecy through typology in the Old
Testament; but the type is never devoid of historical reality:
it belongs to the covenant history of Israel which in its totality
is typological, prophetic of greater things to come in the
redemptive counsel of God.

In saying that the prophetic emphasis is primarily on the
redemptive experience of Israel as a people we do not rule out
the redemptive experience of the individual. The individual
is included in the nation, and the redemption of the nation
involves the individual. The collective aspect of redemption
is more prominent in the Old Testament, just as the personal
or individual aspect is more prominent in the New; but in
neither case does the one exclude the other. There is a very
personal note in Jacob's blessing of the sons of Joseph:

> "*The God before whom my fathers Abraham and Isaac walked,*
>   *the God who has led me all my life long to this day,*
>   *the angel who has redeemed me from all evil—.*"
>   (Genesis 48:15-16)

The same is true of the testimony of the psalmist,

> *For thou hast delivered my soul from death,*
>   *my eyes from tears,*
>   *my feet from stumbling;*
> *I walk before the Lord*
>   *in the land of the living.* (Psalm 116:8-9)

The frequently expressed faith in God as Redeemer and Saviour in every time of need, the very theology of redemption with its two facets: God the Redeemer and the redeemed people, witness to a ceaseless redemptive activity of Him who is faithful to His covenant and to His people.

The historical contemporaneity of this redemption is obvious: God acts in given historical situations, in concrete instances of trouble, in reference to definite human needs; but the eschatological significance of it all is, it would seem, just as obvious: the individual mountain peaks of redemptive experience rise ever higher and higher and point in themselves *as interpreted by the prophets and the apostles* to the times of restoration of all things (Acts 3:21, ASV),[15] to the day of "earth's redemption."

The covenant background for this redemptive interpretation of history, whether it be the national history of Israel or the personal history of the believer, is unmistakable. The Exodus redemption is in fulfilment of the promise to Abraham. "And God heard their groaning, and God remembered his covenant with Abraham, with Isaac, and with Jacob" (Exodus 2:24). The redemption from Babylon is in fulfilment of the same gracious covenant purpose of God with His people:

> *But now thus says the Lord,*
>   *he who created you, O Jacob,*
>   *he who formed you, O Israel:*
> *Fear not, for I have redeemed you;*
>   *I have called you by name, you are mine.* (Isaiah 43:1)

---

[15] *American Standard Version* of the Holy Bible.

The psalmist reflects a covenant-motivated faith in God as his redeemer when he prays,

> *Let the words of my mouth and the meditation of my heart*
> *be acceptable in thy sight,*
> *O Lord, my rock and my redeemer.* (Psalm 19:14)

It is because God is faithful to His covenant that the believer is sure of his redemption.

The eschatological implications of the redemptive acts of God in Israel's history are an important part of the prophetic interpretation. We are reminded once more of the shortened perspective of prophecy, which blends past, present, and future into one picture: redemption is seen as an experience in the past, as an experience that is near at hand, as an experience that is oft repeated, as an experience in the future that is related to the time of the end. It is because of this eschatological implication of redemption that the New Testament rightly understands it as prophetic of Jesus Christ. The redemption in Christ is seen to be the beautiful fruition of God's purpose with Israel as His servant and to find its most significant expression in the commission to the Church to preach the gospel. For ultimately it is the gospel of Jesus Christ which alone is the power of God for salvation to every one who has faith, to the Jew first and also to the Greek (Romans 1:16). From the viewpoint of Christian faith the goal of all God's redemptive activity is reached when we can confidently confess, "In him (that is, in Christ) we have redemption through his blood, the forgiveness of our trespasses according to the riches of his grace which he lavished upon us" (Ephesians 1:7, 8). And yet, even Christian faith *looks forward* in confident hope of something still to come; for as Paul also says, "we wait for adoption as sons, the redemption of our bodies" (Romans 8:23). Redemption from sin and death is the goal; but every redemptive act of God in human experience has foreshadowed and prepared the way for the coming of this final glorious redemption which is in Christ and by Christ alone.

God moves towards His covenant goal by acts of judgment and of redemption. Each judgment experience, each redemptive act, brings the people of God closer to the goal, "the time for establishing all that God spoke by the mouth of his holy prophets from of old" (Acts 3:21, RSV).

VIII. Eyes on the Goal

If we are correct in our conclusions thus far we can readily see the importance in our interpretation of Old Testament prophecy of keeping our eyes on the goal, and on God who will not fail in attaining to that goal.

We are reminded of Peter on the lake of Gennesaret, when on the invitation of his Master he got out of the boat and walked on the water to come to Jesus. All went well as long as he looked at the Lord who bade him come; but "when he saw the wind, he was afraid" and began to sink. His eyes wavered from the goal and from Him who had said, "Come!" Then there was fear.

We are reminded of Paul with his inspired words, "I press on toward the goal for the prize of the upward call of God in Christ Jesus" (Philippians 3:14). From the moment of his conversion to the moment of his death there is a singleness of purpose about Paul that is expressed in this same chapter when he says, "one thing I do." Paul had his eyes on the goal set before him by his faith in Jesus Christ. With his eyes on the goal there was no fear, even though his way led through much suffering for the sake of Christ's name.

We are reminded of the psalmist, who almost lost his faith when he looked at the seeming success of the wicked and arrogant in this world. He admits that his feet "had almost

stumbled" and his steps "had well nigh slipped" because of
envy of the prosperity of the wicked and from faintheartedness
in the face of the affliction of God's people. But he found the
answer to his fears when he looked at the goal and fixed his
eyes on God, who had set the goal before him by His gracious
covenant promises and by His mighty redemptive acts in
behalf of His people in the past. His words are worth quoting
at some length:

> *But when I thought how to understand this,*
>   *it seemed to me a wearisome task,*
> *until I went into the sanctuary of God;*
>   *then I perceived their end.*
> *Truly thou dost set them in slippery places;*
>   *thou dost make them fall to ruin.*
>
> *Nevertheless I am continually with thee;*
>   *thou dost hold my right hand.*
> *Thou dost guide me with thy counsel,*
>   *and afterward thou wilt receive me to glory.*
> *Whom have I in heaven but thee?*
>   *And there is nothing upon earth that I desire besides thee.*
> *My flesh and my heart may fail,*
>   *but God is the strength of my heart and my portion for ever.*
>   (Psalm 73:16-18, 23-26)

The New Testament statement of faith and hope is not essentially different: "I consider that the sufferings of this present
time are not worth comparing with the glory that is to be
revealed to us" (Romans 8:18ff.).

In what we have been saying there is no thought of limiting the prophetic message or the Christian faith to an other-
worldliness that ignores the privilege, the opportunity, the
responsibility, the eternal significance, if you will, of *today*
in relation to tomorrow, of the way in which we walk in
relation to the goal we seek. That would be to misinterpret
completely both Old Testament prophecy and the New Testament gospel. But in urging God's people to live faithfully,

and even joyfully, the life on earth, which in its very nature
is a good gift of God, the prophets would remind us of certain fundamental truths that we need to keep before our
eyes.

We need to see clearly in whom we have put our trust.
The Old Testament prophets picture Him as "God the Redeemer," who is mighty to save; the One who redeemed
Israel from the house of bondage in Egypt (Micah 6:4), and
from captivity in Babylon (Isaiah 44:23ff.), the One with
whom there is "plenteous redemption" and who will redeem
His people "from all their iniquities" (Psalm 130:7, 8; cf. Acts
3:26). The New Testament presents the completed picture:
the full glory of God the Redeemer, who through Christ
has redeemed us from sin and death and has given the hope
of eternal life. The burden of the Christian confession is
this: "Through him you have confidence in God, who raised
him from the dead and gave him glory, so that your faith
and hope are in God." (I Peter 1:21) But that is the burden
of the prophetic message too: "that your faith and hope might
be in God" (ASV). To keep our eyes on God is to keep our
eyes on the goal in the reading of prophecy.

We need to see clearly what God the Redeemer, who is
also the God of the covenant, has really promised. For example, in Exodus 19:5-6. "Now therefore if you will obey my
voice and keep my covenant, you shall be my own possession
among all peoples; for all the earth is mine, and you shall be
to me a kingdom of priests and a holy nation." The conditional form of the promise is unmistakable. God seeks faith
and obedience from the people that He calls in love to be
His *segullah,* "mine own treasure" (AJV),[16] "my own prized
possession" (Moffatt),[17] "my own possession" (RSV),[18] "my

---

[16] *American Jewish Version,* 1917.
[17] James Moffatt, *A New Translation of the Bible,* 1950.
[18] Revised Standard Version, 1952.

very own" (Smith-Goodspeed).[19] The glorious content of the promise is that by faith which is obedient we may have fellowship with Him as our God and experience His redemptive acts in behalf of His people; a deliverance ultimately from all manner of evil, as Luther says in his explanation to the last petition in the Lord's Prayer. Immanuel, God with us, is the very heart of the prophetic word to God's people who truly seek Him. The manner, or the time, of His deliverance is of less importance than the assurance of His presence, and the confidence that He who promised is faithful. To keep our eyes on this central idea in the divine promise, His presence, is to keep our eyes also on the goal in reading prophecy.

We need to see clearly that God is moving towards the goal of His promises, the full realization of His gracious presence with His people, by acts of judgment and of redemption. It isn't so important that Scripture should predict every time and each situation in which God acts in this way. It is important that we share the prophetic faith that this is the way in which God does act, not once but repeatedly. It is not important to "prove" that Scripture is true because it "predicts" events centuries before they happen. It is important to "interpret" events when they take place in the light of the prophetic message of the God who acts continually in judgment and in redemption. It isn't so important to be able to "identify" the enemies of God's kingdom in terms of some specific prophecy, and to "announce" what is about to happen in our own day on the basis of some "proof" passage from the prophets. It is important that we search our hearts to know whether we really belong to the people of God or not; and if we do, to have confidence in God.

If we read prophecy from this point of view we will be less fearful of the strong winds that blow in the ofttime strange

---

[19] J. M. Powis Smith, Edgar J. Goodspeed, *An American Translation of the Bible*, 1939.

history of man on earth: we will find that prophecy has a special message of hope and encouragement for an age of fear, a message which is closely related to the gospel which through Christ becomes the fulfilment of prophecy.

Conclusion

We return to our theme of prophecy for an Age of Fear.

What is the relevance of Old Testament prophecy for today? How shall we understand it? How shall we use it? How shall we interpret it when we preach? What message does it have for men already "fainting with fear and with foreboding of what is coming on the world" (Luke 21:26)? How does it relate to the good news of the gospel?

1. From the negative side, there are at least four ways in which prophecy should not be used.

a. It should never be used with the aim of satisfying human curiosity. It is not a means of divination. It is not history written before the event. It must not be reduced to the level of tea-leaves, by which some would seek to have their future foretold. It is fundamentally and irrevocably religious in its purpose. It has to do with the life of faith and the future of the kingdom of God. Its true purpose is to pass judgment on all human conduct, and especially the conduct of the people of God, and on human history itself, in the light of God's revealed will; and then through repentance to lead on to renewed faith and hope in God who is faithful to the covenant of blessing first made with Abraham, and then confirmed to Israel, and finally received by the Gentiles also in Christ Jesus our Lord.

b. It should never be used in the attempt to determine "times and seasons." It is not a time-chart, as if we could establish an itinerary and a calendar for the future acts of God. "It is not for you to know times or seasons which the Father has fixed by his own authority," said Jesus to the disciples (Acts 1:7). That is plain speech which none should misunderstand. The whole theology of the Old Testament supports it. The living God did not send the prophets to put Him into the strait jacket of human calendars or charts by their predictions of "the latter days." He sent them with a message of judgment on all who "do not obey the truth" (Romans 2:8) and with a message of hope "for every one who does good" (Romans 2:10); and this is the message of the prophets also for us today.

c. It should never be used with reckless disregard of the historically contemporaneous situation, in the attempt to "identify" some modern man or nation in terms of predictive prophecy. For example, when the eighth century prophets, Amos, Hosea, Isaiah, Micah, speak of Assyria they mean the Assyrian empire of their day. In what we may call its "representative" capacity what is said of Assyria, both as the rod of God's anger for the chastisement of His people (Isaiah 10) and as the enemy of God's people whose downfall is predicted (Nahum), may indeed apply to many a situation and many a nation since then, and may have its counterpart in our own day; but that is quite different from saying that the prophets spoke not of Assyria, let us say, but of modern Russia. If the prophecy applies also to the twentieth century, if it foreshadows something that will characterize the very "end of the age," it is not because of some strange gift of soothsaying in the prophet but rather because of his firm and true faith in that "clear continuity of theological principle" which gives the assurance that God can always be depended on to act "in character," acting in judgment or in redemption as befits the situation.

d. It should never be used without keeping firmly in mind its relation to the fulfilment of the central idea in the covenant with Abraham and with Israel. Did Jesus Christ "fulfil" the law and the prophets? He himself says that he did (Matthew 5:17). Did the covenant of blessing made with Abraham and his seed include the Gentiles? The apostle Paul says that it did (Galatians 3:14). Did the new covenant make the old covenant obsolete because all that was of permanent value in it was taken up into the new? The writer of Hebrews 8:13 would answer Yes. May we apply to the New Testament people of God, the Church which is the body of Christ, and in which there is no distinction between Jew and Gentile, the promises given originally to God's Old Testament people Israel? The voice of the New Testament is surely affirmative. The very principle of "fulfilment" in redemptive history demands that we say Yes. Are we right in accepting the more spiritual concept of the kingdom of God and of salvation in the New Testament as a continuation and consummation of what the prophets say about the same themes in the more earthly "times-coloring" of the Old Testament situation? Is there at the same time *unity* and *progression* in the Scriptures of the Old and the New Testament? Christian faith accepts the New Testament answer which is an emphatic affirmative. All this simply illustrates the necessity of interpreting prophecy in close harmony with the whole Biblical truth of the divine covenant with men. Then even chapters such as Ezekiel 38 and 39, where fanciful interpretation has so often had a field day, are seen to speak this single truth of a final victory of God and of the final glorious consummation of His covenant with His people. Who are Gog and Magog? No one can identify them with certainty; but who can miss their significance? They represent the concentrated enmity and fury of the kingdoms of the world against the kingdom of God; and the ultimate victory which the prophecy declares, a victory that issues in the permanent restoration and spiritual renewal of Israel, foreshadows the victory of which we read in Revelation 11:15, "The kingdom of the world has become the kingdom of our Lord and of his Christ, and he shall reign for ever and ever."

2. From the positive side we could say much more; though much of it is repetition and summary.

A right interpretation and use of Old Testament prophecy should lead to repentance. John the Baptist stood in the line of succession to the prophets when he came preaching in the wilderness of Judea, "Repent, for the kingdom of heaven is at hand" (Matthew 3:1-2). So did Jesus, who by his own claim came to fulfil the law and the prophets, and who "began to preach" with identically the same words as John (Matthew 4:17). Prophecy would have us view every historical situation, and certainly then also our own in this twentieth century A.D., in the light of God's judgments. But why? Fear is indeed one of the divine objectives; but it is the fear of God, which is the beginning of wisdom (Proverbs 9:10; Psalm 111:10): it is the "godly grief" that "produces a repentance that leads to salvation and brings no regret" (II Corinthians 7:10). We speak now of repentance on both the personal and the national level. We speak especially of the Christian man and the Christian Church, whose function in an age of fear is to be the voice of conscience bidding all men to repentance. If our generation had a little more fear of God there would be less need to fear men. A right use of prophecy will move us to the right kind of fear; even as Jesus said, "And do not fear those who kill the body but cannot kill the soul; rather fear him who can destroy both soul and body in hell" (Matthew 10:28).

A right interpretation and use of Old Testament prophecy

should lead also to a firm faith in the living God, and therefore to a confident hope in the ultimate victory of good over
evil, the eventual triumph of righteousness, and the final
coming of His kingdom: a coming which the prophets foretold and for which our Lord Jesus taught us to pray. Obadiah
speaks for all the prophets when he says, "The kingdom shall
be the Lord's" (verse 21). Isaiah too speaks for them all when
he says,

> *Of the increase of his government and of peace*
> * there will be no end,*
> *upon the throne of David, and over his kingdom,*
> * to establish it, and to uphold it*
> *with justice and with righteousness*
> * from this time forth and forevermore.*
> *The zeal of the Lord of hosts will do this.*
>
> (Isaiah 9:7)

Thy kingdom come! We may well ask whether we as Christians really believe that it will; that it is coming now into
the hearts and lives of men who truly receive Jesus Christ
as Saviour and Lord, and that its final victory is assured by
the promise of the living God. A right understanding of
prophecy will strengthen this faith of the Christian *in God*
even in an age of fear.

> *Strengthen the weak hands,*
> * and make firm the feeble knees.*
> *Say to those who are of a fearful heart,*
> * "Be strong, fear not!*
> *Behold, your God*
> * will come with vengeance,*
> *with the recompense of God.*
> * He will come and save you."* (Isaiah 35:3-4)

> *But you, Israel, my servant,*
> * Jacob, whom I have chosen,*
> * the offspring of Abraham, my friend;*

you whom I took from the ends of the earth,
  and called from its farthest corners,
saying to you, "You are my servant,
  I have chosen you and not cast you off";
fear not, for I am with you,
  be not dismayed, for I am your God;
I will strengthen you, I will help you,
  I will uphold you with my victorious right hand.
                                        (Isaiah 41:8-10)

If you hesitate to claim this "fear not" of prophecy for God's people today, if the letter of it makes you think of national Israel and not of the Christian Church, if it seems to belong wholly to the past and not to the present, will you read what Paul says in the third chapter of Galatians: "So you see that it is men of faith who are the sons of Abraham.—And if you are Christ's, then you are Abraham's offspring, heirs according to promise" (verses 7 and 29). It is along this line that we establish the relevant connection between the "Fear not" of the prophets and the "Fear not" of Jesus.

A right interpretation and use of Old Testament prophecy should lead to peace; an inner peace that passes all understanding (compare Isaiah 26:3 and Philippians 4:7); but also the confident hope that "peace on earth" among men is not an illusion but a God-given goal to be sought and won, for He is faithful who has promised. The prophets speak often of peace as if it were the ultimate goal of God's covenant with men. They do not presume to tell in minute detail when and how it will come, but they are sure that it will come. The Wonder-child that is to be born is pre-eminently the Prince of Peace, and "of the increase of his government and of peace there will be no end" (Isaiah 9:7). "I will make a covenant of peace with them," says the Lord by His prophet Ezekiel (34:25; 37:26); and through Isaiah He says,

Then justice will dwell in the wilderness,
  and righteousness abide in the fruitful field.
And the effect of righteousness will be peace,
  and the result of righteousness, quietness and trust for ever.
My people will abide in a peaceful habitation,
  in secure dwellings, and in quiet resting places.
                                        (Isaiah 32:16-18)

In the latter days, says Micah,

He shall judge between many peoples,
  and shall decide for strong nations afar off;
and they shall beat their swords into plowshares,
  and their spears into pruning hooks;
nation shall not lift up sword against nation,
  neither shall they learn war any more;
but they shall sit every man under his vine, and under his fig tree,
  and none shall make them afraid;
for the mouth of the Lord of hosts has spoken.
                                        (Micah 4:3-4)

We rightly believe that Jesus Christ is "our peace," and that this peace in its origin and essence is not of this world; but we believe also that He shall reign one day as Prince of Peace over a redeemed and restored humanity. The Old Testament prophets can strengthen us in this faith even in an age of fear where peace seems so remote from reality.

A right interpretation and use of Old Testament prophecy should lead also to a quiet faithfulness to duty while we watch and wait for the redemptive acts of God that will usher in the reign of peace. For the future hope does not excuse the Christian believer from his responsibility in an evil world and in an age of fear. We speak now not only of his duty to proclaim the gospel. That comes first; for without the gospel of Christ, which is the power of God for salvation, there is no dynamic that can cope with the dilemma in which sinful men find themselves even in terms of this present life, nor is there any future hope for a peace based upon righteousness. But we speak also of the responsibility that rests in a special way upon us as Christians to translate faith into action; to seek peace, and the things which make for peace, among men and nations; to seek with passionate earnestness that righteousness of life without which there can be no peace on earth. Micah speaks for all the prophets when he says,

> *He has showed you, O man, what is good;*
> *and what does the Lord require of you*
> *but to do justice, and to love kindness,*
> *and to walk humbly with your God?* (Micah 6:8)

If with the prophets we were more concerned to promote these divine requirements for God's people we would have less need for human fears, which are a result of the disregard of these requirements by our fellowmen for whom we have a peculiar responsibility if we really belong to the people of God.

A right interpretation and use of Old Testament prophecy should lead to a clear, calm, courageous evaluation of the foe, the forces of evil arrayed against God and against His people. It is a formidable foe. It is formidable even if we think only of the conflict between the "free world" and the tyranny of dictators imbued with the cruel fanaticism of communist ideology; but Paul has given a still more fearsome evaluation of the nature of the foe and of his strength in Ephesians 6:12, "For we are not contending against flesh and blood, but against the principalities, against the powers, against the world rulers of this present darkness, against the spiritual hosts of wickedness in the heavenly places." It is against the background of such a picture of the power of the enemy that we must understand the quiet word of assurance given by Jesus to His disciples in every age, "I have said this to you, that in me you may have peace. In the world you have tribulation; but be of good cheer, I have overcome the world"

(John 16:33). Do we believe it, in the sense of that confidence which has enabled Christian martyrs to stand fast in the faith even unto death? Do we believe it, in the sense of the confidence so often voiced by the prophets in the final consummation of God's covenant of peace in an earth "reborn"?

A right interpretation and use of Old Testament prophecy should lead to a clear-sighted recognition that the battle lines in human history are drawn now as they always have been in accordance with the simple preview given in the Protevangelium, when God said,

> *I will put enmity between you and the woman,*
> *and between your seed and her seed;*
> *he shall bruise your head,*
> *and you shall bruise his heel.* (Genesis 3:15)

In that conflict our Captain now as always is God the King, and him whom He has sent, the Lord Jesus Christ our Saviour, the Lord of lords and the King of kings. When Joshua saw a man with a drawn sword in his hand standing near Jericho he asked him, "Are you for us, or for our adversaries?" (Joshua 5:13) The answer went beyond the question. It was more than a reaffirmation of the covenant truth "God with us"; a truth that runs like one unified promise through all of Scripture and reaches glorious heights in Romans 8:31ff. and in Revelation 21:3ff. It was a claim to leadership in the battle: "No, but as commander of the army of the Lord I have now come" (Joshua 5:14). It is so still today. Therefore we are urged to fix "our gaze upon Jesus, the Leader and Perfecter of faith" (Weymouth, Hebrews 12:2).[20]

In that conflict our assurance now as always is in the ultimate victory of God and of His kingdom. What we dare hope for is the final triumph of good over evil under the victorious

---

[20] Richard Francis Weymouth, *The New Testament in Modern Speech*, 4th ed., 1924.

banner of our God. This assurance the prophets had, and we are inspired by their words to share their faith. "The kingdom shall be the Lord's" (Obadiah 21). "The kingdom of the world has become the kingdom of our Lord and of his Christ, and he shall reign for ever and ever" (Revelation 11:15). The Lord God omnipotent reigneth!

In that conflict our insight is clear as to one fundamental truth: that God is not absent from but active in human history, and that He moves towards the goal of His covenant by judgments and by acts of redemption, and that the manner in which the two are blended in human experience is in His hands until in His own good time the goal is reached. In this the prophets and the apostles agree: It will be reached! The kingdom of God will come! The dominion shall be the Lord's in the end, however violently it may be challenged now. "The Lord is the everlasting God, the Creator of the ends of the earth" (Isaiah 40:28), and His promise of redemption is sure. He will not fail. Such is the message of the prophets for God's people in an age of fear.

"Now when these things begin to take place, look up and raise your heads, because your redemption is drawing near" (Luke 21:28).

Israel's Biblical Basis
for Claiming
the Holy Land

Introduction

We restate our theme in the form of a question. Does Israel have a Biblical basis for claiming the Holy Land today?

To some Christians the question may seem to be quite irrelevant religiously. To others, however, it is a vital issue in Biblical interpretation, and especially in the interpretation of predictive prophecy. The re-establishment of Israel as a political state in the land of Palestine has naturally focussed the attention of the Bible reader upon the future of Israel and the significance of the original promise of a land. Does this land belong to Israel by divine right today? Recently the question was debated in *Christianity Today* by O. T. Allis and Wilbur Smith, both lifelong students of Scripture, with the former giving a negative and the latter an affirmative answer. Whether our own answer be Yes or No we should be ready to give a reason for and a defense of our conviction on the basis of Scripture.

Will you note that the scope of our discussion is strictly

defined by the three words "a Biblical basis." It is not our purpose to enter into a discussion of the political aspects of the Palestinian problem, where emotional sympathies and ethical considerations complicate a situation that would challenge the wisdom of a Solomon to find a solution that is just and fair to all concerned. I recall reading somewhere that the greatest tragedy in life is not where right is overcome by wrong, for that may be rectified by the turn of events, and men can live in hope of eventual vindication; but when two equally valid rights conflict, and there is no solution without injustice and suffering for someone, that is tragedy. The *Christian Century* puts it well in its issue for March 6, 1957: "What do you hope in a situation where the problem is precisely the head-on clash of absolutely contrary hopes?" Ideally there could be one solution; and it is not the victory of Arab over Jew, or of Jew over Arab, but the victory of the love of Christ in the hearts of both. The love of Christ could find a way, because it thinks first of the welfare of others; and "mercy triumphs over judgment," even the judgment which says, "This is mine, not yours."

May I say a further word also about the two articles by Allis and Smith in *Christianity Today* for December 24, 1956, which suggested our theme. It will not take you long to discover, if you read the articles, that my convictions are on the side of Allis and not of Smith. Smith does point up the question for us in his opening paragraph. It states the issue clearly as far as it goes. That it does not go far enough becomes clear from the article itself; for from his treatment of the Old Testament we can see that there is involved a basic difference of opinion as to fundamental principles of Old Testament interpretation. What that difference is I hope to make clear as we examine the Scriptures. What does God say? How do you read?

I. *The Covenant with Abraham*

Our first problem is to understand the covenant with Abraham and the terms of the call to him as stated in Gen. 12:1-3.

"Now the Lord said to Abram, 'Go from your country and your kindred and your father's house to the land that I will show you. And I will make of you a great nation, and I will bless you, and make your name great, so that you will be a blessing. I will bless those who bless you, and him who curses you I will curse; and by you all the families of the earth will bless themselves (or, in you all the families of the earth will be blessed).'"

There are four significant elements in this statement of divine purpose with respect to Abraham. Each is repeated and reaffirmed and clarified as we move through the book of Genesis, and through the Old Testament, and even into the New; each is related to Abraham's vocation and to the covenant that God made with him.

The first is the command to leave country and kindred, and to separate himself unto God's calling and purpose for him. What that calling and purpose was we shall see in a moment. It ought to be clear from the start that it meant more than leaving one country for another. There is more involved than geographical considerations. The sequel makes it clear that this was a religious experience, which involved commitment and consecration; or shall we say, faith and obedience. But faith in whom, and obedience in what?

That becomes clear from the promise that follows. It is a three-fold promise; though one of the three is implied rather than explicitly stated in these opening verses of Genesis 12.

First He promises to Abraham a seed, the Hebrew *zera'*, a singular-collective noun, which can mean either an individual or descendants, in the sense of a family or a nation. The word *seed* (zera') is not found yet (we meet it in 12:7, and often from there on); but God does say, "I will make of you a great nation." There is definitely from the beginning a promise of a seed: a promise which in Gen. 21:12 is attached to Isaac, "for through Isaac shall your descendants be named" (or, "in Isaac shall thy seed be called"); in Isaiah 41:8 to Israel as a nation, "But you, Israel, my servant, Jacob, whom I have chosen, the offspring (or, seed) of Abraham, my friend"; in Galatians 3:16 to Jesus Christ, "Now the promises were made to Abraham and to his offspring. It does not say, 'And to offsprings,' referring to many; but referring to one, 'And to your offspring' (or seed), which is Christ"; and in Galatians 3:29 to every Christian believer, "And if you are Christ's, then you are Abraham's offspring (or seed), heirs according to promise."

There is next the promise of a land: implied in vs. 1, in the command to go "to the land that I will show you," and in vs. 2, in that a great nation must necessarily have a land in which to live; and made specific in vs. 7, "To your descendants I will give this land." Wilbur Smith is probably correct when he says that "God's giving of Palestine to Israel is more frequently referred to than any other act of God toward Israel, even than the deliverance from Egypt or the promise of the Messiah." But does that make the promise of a land the really important thing in the covenant with Abraham, more important than the coming of the Messiah? Two things should be noted: *first*, that the promise of the land does not stand in the climactic position in Gen. 12 (that, as we shall see, is reserved for the promise of blessing), and *second*, that as we trace the reaffirmations of this promise of a land through the Old Testament and into the New it is seen more and more to be a symbol of something greater, something that is not of earth at all. We are reminded of Jesus' words before Pilate, "My kingship (or kingdom) is not of this world; if my kingship were of this world, my servants would fight,

that I might not be handed over to the Jews; but my kingship is not from the world" (John 18:36). And with respect
to the promises to the patriarchs the author of the Epistle to
the Hebrews writes: "These all died in faith, not having received what was promised, but having seen it and greeted
it from afar, and having acknowledged that they were stran-
gers and exiles on the earth. For people who speak thus make
it clear that they are seeking a homeland. If they had been
thinking of that land from which they had gone out, they
would have had opportunity to return. But as it is, they
desire a better country, that is, a heavenly one. Therefore
God is not ashamed to be called their God, for he has prepared for them a city" (Hebrews 11:13-16).

The third facet of the promise to Abraham is that of blessing. It is a promise that God would bless Abraham, but also
that He would make him a blessing, a promise of blessing *to*
and of a blessing *through* this man and his seed. It is the
latter that stands in climactic position in the paragraph. Abraham was called to be a blessing, or, a servant of God through
whom blessing should be mediated to others. The promise
was, "In you shall all the families of the earth be blessed."
Note how the promise is repeated and reaffirmed and related
to the seed and otherwise clarified in Genesis 18:17-18, in
Genesis 22:15-16, in Genesis 26:2-4, and in Genesis 28:13-14.
Note further that it is this promise which in the New Testament is definitely related to Christ: for example, in Acts
3:25-26, "You are the sons of the prophets and of the covenant
which God gave to your fathers, saying to Abraham, 'And in
your posterity shall all the families of the earth be blessed.'
God, having raised up his servant, sent him to you first, to
bless you in turning every one of you from your wickedness";
and also in Galatians 3:8, "And the scripture, foreseeing that
God would justify the Gentiles by faith, preached the Gospel
beforehand to Abraham, saying, 'In thee shall all the nations

be blessed,'" and 3:14, "that in Christ Jesus the blessing of Abraham might come upon the Gentiles, that we might receive the promise of the Spirit through faith."

The important thing is the gospel, not the land; and the blessing of Abraham includes the Gentiles, not only the Jews. The inheritance spoken of is a spiritual, not a material, inheritance. The sons of Abraham, heirs according to promise, are *men of faith* of every race. And in Christ all distinctions are removed, so that there is neither Jew nor Greek, "for you are all one in Christ Jesus" (Gal. 3:28).

Let us return to the promise of the land. How do you read? In the light of the total picture the land is seen to be simply a means to an end, a preparatory step in the realization of God's vocation to Abraham and to his seed to be a blessing. When it had accomplished its purpose in the total plan it could be regarded as fulfilled and set aside. That is true of the whole history of Israel as a nation. Israel was not called to be an end in itself, but a means to an end; to be a servant of God through whom we have received the Sacred Scriptures as the Word of God, and Jesus Christ according to the flesh as the Saviour of the world. Jesus Christ and the Church which is His body is the fulfilment: not an accidental afterthought, but the intended goal from the beginning; the fulfilment of the vocation of Abraham to be a blessing and of Israel to be a kingdom of priests, and a holy nation (Exodus 19:6). Significantly, the very words of the latter passage (Exodus 19:5-6) are applied to the Church in I Peter 2:9-10: "But you are a chosen race, a royal priesthood, a holy nation, God's own people (or, a people for his possession), that you may declare the wonderful deeds of him who called you out of darkness into his marvelous light. Once you were no people but now you are God's people; once you had not received mercy but now you have received mercy." (See also vs. 4-5.) And the words of Paul in Ephesians I concerning "every spiritual blessing in the heavenly places" in Christ, in whom we are "destined and appointed to live for the praise of his glory," with the Holy Spirit as the guarantee of our inheritance in hope "until we acquire possession of it," is more than a superficial reflection of the similar language in the Old Testament: it is the fulfilment of it.

Do you see why we said that our answer to the question in our theme is a matter of fundamental principles of interpretation? Luther made salvation by grace, and justification by faith, and the gospel of Jesus Christ, the key to a right understanding of Scripture. The New Testament is constantly drawing out the deep spiritual implications of that which was said and done, of history and of prophecy, in the Old Testament. In the light of the New Testament the exaggerated emphasis on land and nation instead of on the promise of blessing seems like a religious anachronism. To substitute the millennium for the gospel as the interpretative key to Scripture will save no one, nor will it solve anything. The love of Christ might find a way; a political claim to Palestine based on a faulty Scriptural exegesis never will.

II. The Historical Fulfilment of Prophecy

There is another aspect of this promise of a land that needs to be considered.

Prophecy is an integral part of Old Testament history, and in interpreting prophecy we must see it first in its own historical situation. Interpretation begins with the historically contemporaneous aspect of the prophecy. It may be that it does not project beyond the immediate historical situation. It may be that it has found an adequate fulfilment in the past. If it projects into the future the interpretation must take into consideration the progressiveness of revelation and reinterpret in the light thereof.

When God said to Abraham in Genesis 12:7, "To your descendants I will give this land," a promise spelled out in greater detail in Genesis 15:18-21 and repeated many times between the call of Abraham and the covenant with Israel at Sinai, the promise belonged within what we may call *the Exodus situation*, the beginnings of the Hebrew nation. Just as the promise of a numerous seed had been fulfilled in Egypt, so the promise of a land was fulfilled when Israel conquered and possessed Canaan under Joshua. Joshua refers to it in his farewell message to his people as "this good land which the Lord your God has given you" (Joshua 23:15). There is no need of looking beyond that fulfilment as far as the original promise is concerned. God kept His promise to give the land. The promise in Genesis and Exodus must be understood in its historical context.

But after 500 years of possession of the land Israel was again dispossessed. The reason we shall discuss later, and it too has a significant bearing on our theme. When, however, Israel went into exile, the Northern Kingdom (for Israel was divided now) into the Assyrian Captivity in 722 B.C., and the Southern Kingdom into the Babylonian Captivity in 586 B.C., the prophets who predicted the captivity began also to predict a return from captivity.

In these prophecies of a return the land naturally figures again. It cannot be said that it is the most prominent part of the prophetic promise. There is a deepening spiritual note, which makes it clear that the essential part of the experience is a return unto God; a renewal of the covenant experience of blessing through forgiveness to a people now ready to respond to God's *hesed* (or steadfast love) with the obedience of faith. Hosea gives a good description of this experience in chapter 2:14-20. Look it up and read it in your Bible. Other prophecies could be added that speak in the same vein. The primary emphasis is not on the land; but the promise of the land is included. "The city shall be rebuilt upon its mound, and the palace shall stand where it used to be," says Jeremiah (30:18); and again "your children shall come back to their own country" (31:17).

The classic passage is the one in Jer. 29:10-14: "For thus says the Lord: When seventy years are completed for Babylon, I will visit you, and I will fulfil to you my promise and bring you back to this place. For I know the plans I have for you, says the Lord, plans for welfare and not for evil, to give you a future and a hope. Then you will call upon me and come and pray to me, and I will hear you. You will seek me and find me; when you seek me with all your heart, I will be found by you, says the Lord, and I will restore your fortunes and gather you from all the nations and all the places where I have driven you, says the Lord, and I will bring you back to the place from which I sent you into exile." Closely parallel is the passage in Isaiah 52:7-12. We could multiply passages like these from the prophets who lived in anticipation of or actually partook in the Babylonian Captivity. They shall return. God will perform a new Exodus-redemption, a new thing. They shall again possess the land and dwell therein as God's people.

The promise is explicit; but from the external point of view all this happened in the return from the Babylonian Captivity. From the external point of view the prophecy (spoken by many men) was fulfilled; and that includes certainly the promise of the land. If there is an unfulfilled element in the prophecies of Isaiah and of Jeremiah and of Ezekiel, and there most certainly is, it would seem to be not in the area of these external things but in the failure to achieve the spiritual reality that was the goal of the covenant. Of that even the prophets were aware, and their awareness is reflected in their message. Their concern is not primarily with Israel's possession of the land, but with a spiritual rebirth of Israel as a true covenant nation, rightly called the people of God, and with the ultimate spiritual fulfilment of their God-given calling to be a blessing in the earth. That is why Jeremiah begins to speak about a new covenant (31:31-34), and Ezekiel about a new heart and new spirit (11:19-20; 18:31; 36:26), and Isaiah about new heavens and a new earth (chapters 65, 66). That is what we mean by progressiveness of revelation: a deepening insight into the spiritual purpose of God's covenant, and therefore into the spiritual nature of the ultimate consummation of the covenant. But as for the promise of a return to the land, that was fulfilled in that historical situation.

III. *The Ultimate Goal of Prophecy*

This leads us to another aspect of prophecy that must be kept clearly in mind. It is the eschatological implication that is found in all of prophecy, even in that which seems to be limited to the immediate historical situation.

We must not minimize either the historically contemporaneous or the eschatological significance of prophecy. I speak as one who has the firm conviction that from the covenant with Abraham and on (perhaps from Gen. 3:15 and on) God in every act and word related to the covenant is looking towards a consummation, is moving towards a goal. What happened in the case of Abraham had significance for him, and for "the times of restoration of all things" of which we read in Acts 3:21 (ASV). The same is true of Israel as a nation. It is true of individuals and institutions within Israel: of Moses, and Samuel, and David, and the prophets; of the priesthood, and the kingship, and what is called in German "das Prophetentum"; of the deliverance from Egypt and of the return from the Babylonian Captivity. The Old Testament is not, as Sellin rightly says, a chain of words of God strung together in a row ("Das A. T. ist keine Kette von aneinandergereihten

Worten Gottes"), but the Word of God in it resembles the treasure hidden in the field; and as a spade with which to dig it up (or draw it out) we have only the Gospel of Christ.[21] That is another way of saying that it is unified from beginning to end by the gospel, or by the redemptive purpose of God. Therefore the question must ever be, "In what way does this word, this promise, this experience, this historic event, relate to, and prepare for, and in a real sense foreshadow the ultimate fulfilment of God's redeeming purpose, of His saving will?"

That holds true of the promise of the land. We have already seen that it had a preparatory significance in relation to the history of Israel as God's servant which has been fulfilled. Does it have also an eschatological significance which points beyond the Exodus situation and beyond the Babylonian Captivity? I believe it does. But what is that significance? If the New Testament writers, anticipating the fall of Jerusalem to the armies of Rome under Titus and the new dispersion of the Jews to the ends of the earth, had done what the prophets did and had spoken of another return to the rocky land of Palestine, I could see a place for the land in the still unfinished plan of God today. But they do not so speak. It is not in the New Testament that you find the promise of the restoration to the land on which the Zionists base their claims to the land. Rather, Jesus says, "My kingdom is not of this world." The new covenant is seen and spoken of as essentially, and even exclusively, spiritual in nature and content. The book of Revelation speaks about a new Jerusalem, but the description is not that of the city in Palestine. In the new Jerusalem there is not even a temple, "for its temple is the Lord God the Almighty and the Lamb" (Rev. 21:22); i.e., the symbol and the shadow has given way to ultimate reality. Even the dis-

---

[21] Ernst Sellin, *Das A. T. im Christlichen Gottesdienst und Unterricht,* 1936, p. 20.

puted millennial picture in Revelation 20 does not speak of the land so much as it does of *the earth*. Smith is quite correct in saying that apart from the belief in a millennial reign of Christ "there is little need to discuss the prophecies regarding the future of Palestine, for it certainly will have no role apart from the Messiah."[22] But what right have we to incorporate Old Testament promises of the land which can be otherwise explained into the millennial picture when the New Testament itself does not do so (except perhaps for the reference to a siege of "the beloved city")?[23] We have spoken before of the fulfilment of the promise of the land in the Exodus from Egypt and in the return from Babylon. If there is a deeper eschatological significance, as I believe there is, it points rather to the "better country, that is, a heavenly one" of Hebrews 11 than to the thousand year reign of Revelation 20: i.e., it points to the ultimate consummation and not to a temporary interlude.

IV. *The Terminology of Prophecy*

But what shall we say of the language of the Old Testament in this matter of the land? If we believe in prophecy, as I do, can we do full justice to the promises by this twofold emphasis on the historically contemporaneous, which has been fulfilled, and on the eschatological, which looks to an ultimate consummation?

What shall we say, for instance, of the terminology in Gen. 17:7-8? "And I will establish my covenant between me and you and your descendants after you throughout their generations for an everlasting covenant, to be God to you and to your descendants after you. And I will give to you, and to your descendants after you, the land of your sojournings, all

---

[22] Wilbur Smith, *Christianity Today*, Dec. 24, 1956.
[23] Revelation 20:9.

the land of Canaan, for an everlasting possession; and I will be their God." Observe that it speaks not only of an everlasting covenant, *berith 'olam,* but of an everlasting possession of the land, *achuzath 'olam:* God promises to give the land "for an everlasting possession." Does not that imply that the entire content of the covenant with Abraham, the promise of land, seed, and blessing, is equally permanent and abiding, in fact, everlasting? And if we believe that God's Word is true, must we not look for a restoration of the Jews to Palestine even in our day as a fulfilment of this promise of God? Must we not take prophecy literally if we believe in prophecy at all?

Again we ask, How do you read? Is it with an eye to the letter only; do you interpret everything that you read literally? Men do not always speak that way, and yet they expect to be understood. If we insist on literalism in all of prophecy we will run into trouble; and especially so if our literal interpretation does not go beyond the English text.

Let us illustrate briefly.

In Genesis 17 the *berith 'olam,* the everlasting covenant, includes circumcision. We read in vs. 13, "So shall my covenant be in your flesh an everlasting covenant." Would anyone insist that circumcision is an eternally valid and necessary ordinance and sign of the divine covenant? Even in the Old Testament, in Jeremiah and in Deuteronomy, we are told that circumcision of the heart, which implies a purely spiritual experience, is more significant than the external circumcision of the flesh. The New Testament is more explicit still. Paul says in Romans 2:28-29, "For he is not a real Jew who is one outwardly, nor is true circumcision something external and physical. He is a Jew who is one inwardly, and real circumcision is a matter of the heart, spiritual and not literal." In Galatians 5:2-6 he goes further and says, "Now I, Paul, say to you that if you receive circumcision, Christ will be of no advantage to you. I testify again to every man who receives circumcision that he is bound to keep the whole law. You are severed from Christ, you who would be justified by the law; you have fallen away from grace. For through the Spirit, by faith, we wait for the hope of righteousness. For in Christ Jesus neither circumcision nor uncircumcision is of any avail, but faith working through love." Circumcision was not one of the four "necessary things" on which the conference at Jerusalem agreed in the dispute between Jewish and Gentile Christians (Acts 15). And yet the same word, *'olam,* is used of the covenant of circumcision and of the promise of the land of Canaan.

Actually the Hebrew word *'olam* does not mean everlasting; it means indefinite time of long duration, either past or future. If the context permits, or perhaps even demands, it may convey the thought of that which is eternal. For instance, when we read in Genesis 21:33 that the name of God is *"YHWH El 'olam"* we quite correctly translate as "the LORD (YAHWEH), the Everlasting God." God is eternal. We can speak of Him in no other way. The Biblical writer clearly uses 'olam in this sense of eternal when he speaks of God. But in Isaiah 63:11 the days of old, *kol yemey 'olam,* are equated with the days of Moses, "Then he remembered the days of old, of Moses his servant" (see the historical context of the Exodus in vs. 7-14); and in Deuteronomy 15:17 we read of a slave who becomes an *'eved 'olam,* a servant or bondman forever, when it is obvious that it means only a servant for life.

How do you read? In this case it is just a matter of a correct knowledge of the flexibility in the use of words; and perhaps what we have said is sufficient to take care of the too literal interpretation of the English text of the promise of a land to Israel. But there are other "time references" in Scripture, and the problem of "how to read" may be bigger than the study of words. For instance, in Jeremiah 33:17-22 we read of a covenant with David which is commonly believed to have Messianic significance; but the same passage speaks in identical language of a covenant with the Levitical priests. I quote verses 17 and 18: "For thus says the Lord: David shall never lack a man to sit on the throne of the house of Israel, and the Levitical priests shall never lack a man in my presence to offer burnt offerings, to burn cereal offerings, and to make sacrifices forever." The Hebrew for "shall never lack" is *lo yikrath,* which in literal translation would read "shall not be cut off." Furthermore, both covenants are said to be just as sure and permanent as the covenant with Noah ("my covenant with the day and my covenant with the night"), which in Genesis 9 is called a *berith 'olam,* or an everlasting covenant. Now, in the New Testament Jesus is frequently referred to as the Son of David, the Messianic king; and so we can readily see that the covenant promise to David is fulfilled in Christ. He was actually of the house and lineage of David. But how about the covenant with the Levitical priests, which is said to be equally enduring? The writer of the Epistle to the Hebrews speaks of "a change in the priesthood," so that Christ is seen as a priest after the order of Melchizedek; "for it is evident that our Lord was descended from Judah, and in connection with that tribe Moses said nothing about priests" (Hebrews 7:14).

It is evident that the similar language of the two parallel covenants in Jeremiah 33 must be differently understood. How do you read? The truth is that both covenants may be fulfilled in Christ, but in different ways: the one more literally than the other; but in both cases, with a more directly spiritual emphasis than is as yet apparent in Jeremiah. To take all prophecy literally will sometimes lead to misinterpretation of prophecy. A far safer rule to follow is the one that "a prophecy is to be regarded as completely fulfilled when its central idea is fulfilled." Anything beyond that is "ex abundanti." What, then, is the central idea in the covenant promise of a land to Abraham?

V. *The Conditional Aspect of Prophecy*

We shift to still another facet of our theme.

In his article in *Christianity Today* Dr. Allis discusses the conditional aspect of the promise of the land.[24] It is a fact that prophecy is often conditional. Wherever an "if" is attached to a prediction or a promise it is obviously conditional; but a prophecy may be conditional without a clear statement to that effect. Jonah preached to Nineveh, "Yet forty days, and Nineveh shall be overthrown!" (3:4). There is every indication that he preached the word of the Lord. But "the people of Nineveh believed God" and repented (3:5); and we read that "When God saw what they did, how they turned from their evil way, God repented of the evil which he had said he would do to them; and he did not do it" (3:10). A similar instance is the prophecy of Micah in ch. 3:12, when seen in the light of Jeremiah 26:16-19. The prophecy in Micah 3:12 is just as unconditional in form as the one in 1:6. The prophecy against Samaria was literally fulfilled. Not so the one against Jerusalem (unless you lose sight of all historical perspective in reading the book of Micah and refer it to a later day, when Jerusalem was captured by Nebuchadnezzar or by Titus). We are not left to guess, however, for Jeremiah 26:16-19 gives the explanation of what actually happened. King Hezekiah humbled himself under the prophetic preaching: he feared the Lord, and entreated the favor of the Lord, and the Lord repented of the evil which He had pronounced against the nation through His servant Micah. The judgment was averted. The prophecy in Micah 3:12 was a "conditional prophecy."

---

[24] O. T. Allis, *Christianity Today*, Dec. 24, 1956.

It was conditional even though no condition was stated in the prophecy. May that not be true of other predictions as well? In answer to Hölscher's claim that no genuine prophecy has been fulfilled Wilhelm Möller admits that some prophecies are unfulfilled because they were "ethically conditioned" (etiskt betingade).[25] It is as if God would say when He sends His servants to pronounce judgment, "These things shall surely be unless you repent." Sometimes, as in Micah 3:12, He doesn't say it; but He means it just the same. In fact, why should He announce judgment at all, why not send it unannounced, except that God looks for a possible repentance so that He might not need to judge?

But how about the promissory element in prophecy? Is what we have been saying about conditional prophecies true also of God's promises? Would not that destroy the very basis of our confidence in the "hesed," the steadfast love, of God, which makes Him forever faithful to His covenant in spite of the faithlessness of men? Would it not contradict the reassuring words in II Corinthians 1:20, "For all the promises of God find their Yes in him. That is why we utter the Amen through him, to the glory of God"? God is faithful. God is the God of truth (the God of Amen, Isaiah 65:16). Must not faith stake its all on this that He is faithful who has promised, and that His promises are forever true? And as we pose these searching questions we remember that among His promises is also the promise of a land given to Abraham and to his seed.

The point at issue is whether there can be certainty and condition in relation to the same promises of God. I believe there can. God is indeed eternally faithful to His covenant purpose of redemption; and what He set out to do when He called Abraham He has fulfilled in the sending of Jesus Christ.

---

[25] Wilhelm Möller, *Inledning till Gamla Testamentet,* tr. from the German, 1934.

There is nothing conditional about the gospel that would affect its certainty or our confidence. It is the surest thing in the world. But two things need to be said: *1st,* that God does not order human history in such a way that each man or nation is a mere puppet mechanically manipulated on the stage of life; *2nd,* that when God makes a promise He expects the response of the obedience of faith if the individual concerned is to possess the blessing. When God tested Abraham's faith with the command to offer Isaac as a burnt offering, He did not say that if Abraham would be willing to do as commanded He would bless him; and yet, after the event, He said, "By myself I have sworn, says the Lord, because you have done this, and have not withheld your son, your only son, I will indeed bless you—and by your descendants shall all the nations of the earth bless themselves, *because you have obeyed my voice*" (Genesis 22:15-18). May we not say that God promised His blessing to and through men of faith; and that in that sense faith was indeed a condition for the fulfilment of the promise, though the promise itself was faithful and true. In Exodus 19:5-6 the promise is, "If you will obey my voice and keep my covenant, you shall be my own possession among all peoples; for all the earth is mine, and you shall be to me a kingdom of priests and a holy nation." God could not make use of Israel as a kingdom of priests if they persisted in disobedience; nor could blessing be experienced without faith.

We could multiply passages where this sort of an "if" is connected with the statement of a divine promise. In Deuteronomy 28:1 we read, "And if you obey the voice of the Lord your God, being careful to do all his commandments which I command you this day, the Lord your God will set you on high above all the nations of the earth." The promise is clarified in vs. 2: "And all these blessings shall come upon you and overtake you, if you obey the voice of the Lord your God." In 28:15 we see the other side of the picture: "But if you will not obey the voice of the Lord your God or be careful to do all his commandments and his statutes which I command you this day, then all these curses shall come upon you and overtake you." In Deuteronomy 4:29, with forward reference to the day of captivity, we read this promise: "But from there you will seek the Lord your God, and you will find him, if you search after him with all your heart and with all your soul." We have the same sort of "conditional" language in the New Testament, for example in I John 1:9, "If we confess our sins, he is faithful and just, and will forgive our sins and cleanse us from all unrighteousness." We could continue with illustrations; but need we? God is faithful to His Word, but He can get along without us if we are faithless. That is both the glory and the tragedy of Israel. That which God set out to do through Abraham as His servant and through Israel as His people He has fulfilled, and is fulfilling now, through Christ and the Christian Church. It couldn't be made any clearer than it is in Acts 3:17-26. Read it in your Bible. And notice, it does not say a word about the land of Palestine, or even about Israel as a nation, but drives straight to the heart of the promise of blessing.

How do you read? We must learn to distinguish between that which is the very essence of a promise, or its central idea, and that which belongs to the temporary forms of which God made use in bringing the promise to fulfilment. We must learn to distinguish, too, between the eternal and the transient in prophecy. The possession of the land by Israel was an essential stage in the working out of God's covenant of blessing for all men. So was the call of Abraham and the history of the people of Israel. But nowhere in the New Testament is there the slightest indication that these are of the essence of the new covenant. The "central idea" in the Old Testament promise which is fulfilled in Christ is not the promise of a bit of territory on earth. If the New Testament is right in what it says, even the patriarchs saw more clearly than to set their hopes on an earthly Canaan: they looked for a better country, a heavenly one.

VI. *The Times-Coloring of Prophecy*

But is there not in the Old Testament, in the eschatology of the prophets, a clear and compelling picture of both the land and the people of Israel in the consummation at the end of the age (the Hebrew *be 'acherith hayyamim)?* The closing paragraph in Amos 9 comes to mind (vs. 13-15). Look it up and read it. We have a similar picture in Isaiah 60:15-22. And in Ezekiel 37:25-28 we read: "They shall dwell in the land where your fathers dwelt that I gave to my servant Jacob; they and their children and their children's children shall dwell there forever; and David my servant shall be their prince forever. I will make a covenant of peace with them; it shall be an everlasting covenant with them; and I will be their God, and they shall be my people. Then the nations will know that I the Lord sanctify Israel, when my sanctuary is in the midst of them for evermore." And so we could continue. What shall we say of prophecies such as these?

May I point out two things: *1st,* that these prophecies, if they refer ultimately to Israel alone, cannot be equated with a millennium but belong to the final consummation, which to the prophets was always just beyond the horizon of the present experience of judgment because of Israel's sins; and *2nd,* that the prophets may be using what Ed. Riehm calls the "times-coloring" of their own age to portray for us ultimate spiritual realities, which transcend the immediate physical and geographical and national limitations.[26] If we take these prophecies literally we must reinterpret the New Testament doc-

---

[26] Edward Riehm, *Messianic Prophecy*, tr. from German, 2nd ed., 1891, p. 133.

trine of the kingdom of God in Old Testament terms. Perhaps that is what we ought to do (I think not!), but let us at least be clear as to what is involved if we do insist on a literal interpretation, with a primary reference to Israel as a nation.

The New Testament viewpoint would seem to be entirely different. When Amos says, "In that day I will raise up the booth of David that is fallen and repair its breaches, and raise up its ruins, and rebuild it as in the days of old; that they may possess the remnant of Edom and all the nations who are called by my name, says the Lord who does this" (9:11-12), James in Acts 15:15-18 puts it this way (following the Septuagint): "And with this the words of the prophets agree, as it is written,

After this I will return
and I will rebuild the dwelling of David, which has fallen;
I will rebuild its ruins,
and I will set it up,
that the rest of men may seek the Lord,
and all the Gentiles who are called by my name,
says the Lord, who has made these things known from of old.

The difference is significant. The prophet uses what to him must have been a perfectly natural picture of covenant fulfilment in the form of a national conquest of an ancient enemy. It is as if he visualized the incorporation of Edom in Israel as a result of conquest; in this way the blessing of God's covenant would be shared also by them. The New Testament uses the picture of the Gentiles seeking the God of Israel and a share in the blessings of His people. See Isaiah 2:2-4 and Micah 4:1-4. What is the nature of those blessings? A careful study of the covenant will make it clear that even in the case of Israel they were essentially spiritual. Should it then be too difficult to see that when Amos speaks of the mountains dripping sweet wine he may be concerned with more than material prosperity; and that its ultimate reference is to "every spiritual blessing in the heavenly places in Christ"? It belongs to the progressiveness of revelation to bring out the meaning latent in the original promise in and through the fulfilment. The "times-coloring" disappears, or is sloughed off, and the spiritual reality remains, only more clearly discerned as befits the fulfilment. Which is the more important to stress, the promise of the land or of the blessing? Which is the "central idea" in the covenant promise?

VII. The Question Answered

There is much more that could be said. It would be helpful to investigate the whole Biblical concept of "newness"—the new covenant (Jeremiah 31), the new commandment (John 13), the new thing (Isaiah 43), the new song (Psalm 40, Isaiah 42:10), the new heart and the new spirit (Ezekiel 11, 18, 36), the new Jerusalem (Rev. 21:2), the new creation or the new creature (II Corinthians 5:17), the new man or the new nature (Ephesians 4:22-24), the new heavens and the new earth (Isaiah 65-66, Revelation 21:22)—all the way to the triumphal declaration in Revelation 21:5, "Behold, I make all things new!"

But we must return to our question, Does Israel have a Biblical basis for claiming the Holy Land today? For the evangelical Christian, who understands the centrality of the gospel in the interpretation of Scripture, and who has some appreciation of the progressiveness of revelation and therefore of the distinction as well as of the unity between the Old Testament and the New, the answer must be No. Whether she has a moral right to it is another question; but if she does, it is based not on Scripture but on suffering: it is the right of a people that has suffered much in other lands to have a land that they can call their own. Whether she has a political right to it is also another question; if she does, it is based not on ancient but on modern history, not on the promises of God but on human treaties in our own generation. Whether she has a better right to the land in view of the sufferings through which she has passed than do the Arabs who were dispossessed to make room for Israel and now take their turn in suffering is a question that no man can answer. It belongs to the tragedy of the situation in the Middle East of which I spoke at the beginning. We must remember that the Arabs were in Palestine before our first ancestors came to America: and we call this country ours. It is true that God once dispossessed and destroyed the Canaanites to make room for His people Israel; but not until the iniquity of the Amorites was full to overflowing. Have we the right to put Arabs and Amorites in the same class as touching iniquity? And has a people that persists in rejecting the Messiah the right to claim the land while it rejects the vocation to be a blessing?

No, to assert a Biblical basis for Israel's claim to the Holy Land is to distort Scripture.

VIII. *The Future of Israel*

But one question remains.

What about Israel itself? We ask with Paul, "Has God rejected his people?" and we answer with Paul, "By no means!" (Romans 11:1). Christ died for the Jew as well as for the Gentile. There was no intention of excluding the Jews in including the Gentiles in the covenant purpose of God. The gospel of Jesus Christ is for Israel as much as it is for all.

The pathos of it is that they do not yet understand "the things that make for peace" (Luke 19:41). They persist in rejecting their Messiah, the One in whom their vocation to be the servant of the Lord has found its final fulfilment, the One who came *to them first* with the offer of the supreme blessing of God to which all their history had pointed forward. Is that not of greater concern to us than the question of their right to a land?

If the Christian wants to know what his attitude to Israel ought to be let him read Romans 9-11. Begin with Romans 9:1-5; continue with Romans 10:1-4; do not stop until you have read Romans 11:1-6. Is there a future for Israel in God's redemptive plan? I believe there is. Paul holds forth such a hope in Romans 11:25-26, when he says, "Lest you be wise in your own conceits, I want you to understand this mystery, brethren; a hardening has come upon part of Israel, until the full number of the Gentiles come in, and so all Israel will be saved."

But when that day comes I do not believe that it will mean a return to the old but an entrance into the new: an enlistment under the banner of Jesus Christ in the same spiritual sense in which you and I own him as Saviour and Lord, a place side by side with us in that Church to which God has given the same vocation as He once gave to Israel (I Peter 1:9), an experience of every spiritual blessing in Christ and of a service in the gospel which fulfils their original calling to be a kingdom of priests and a holy nation. If that should happen it might well mean for the world what Paul says in Romans 11:15, "For if their rejection means the reconciliation of the world, what will their acceptance mean but life from the dead?"

For this I believe we should work, and hope, and pray; but as far as I can see from the teaching of Scripture, it can be achieved only by preaching the gospel to them in love, not by supporting Zionist propaganda that Palestine belongs to them by divine right.

The Time-Dimensions of Prophecy: Past, Present, Future

Introduction

Prophecy is an important part of Scripture in relation to Christian preaching; but the preaching often "misses the mark" because it does not understand prophecy.

What is Biblical prophecy? What is its purpose? What is its essential nature? What are the hermeneutical principles to guide us in its interpretation? What is the relevance of prophecy, especially Old Testament prophecy, for the age in which we live? How can we as preachers use it rightly and effectively in our preaching? How can we safeguard ourselves against perverting God's prophetic truth by misinterpretation? Must we because of the difficulty and danger involved in interpretation ignore it altogether and stick to the preaching and teaching of New Testament themes; without thereby avoiding the difficulty, for there is prophecy in the New Testament too?

We shall not attempt to give a specific answer to each of the questions raised; but we shall try to say something about the *nature* of prophecy that may shed some light on the other questions as well. We shall do so by considering what we choose to call the Time-Dimension of Prophecy. We shall try to state and to illustrate three time-aspects of prophecy that are vitally significant for our understanding and use of it today.

I. The Time-Dimension of the Present

Let us start with what we may call the Time-Dimension of the Present. That does not mean our age but the prophet's; for the first significance of any prophecy is as a message for the prophet's own age. Every prophecy was "preached" to a definite historical situation, in a manner and in a language which that age could understand. It had religious relevancy for the prophet's own day. In that sense it had what we call "historical contemporaneity."

The assertion that we have made naturally calls for illustration, and for the confirmation that comes by such illustration; but first let us note what is implied by the assertion. It implies:

1st, The significance of the prophet as a preacher, a spokesman for God and an interpreter of His will, to his own generation.

2nd, The importance of knowing as much as possible about the human situation of which the prophet was a part, and to which he was sent as a preacher, and to which he directed his message.

3rd, The necessity of understanding his message first of all in terms of his own historical milieu by which his language and his thought-forms, and even the message itself, are colored. Ed. Riehm refers to it as local "times-coloring" for the prophetic message.[27] We might call it *an awareness of the situation* such as characterizes all good preaching.

---

[27] Edw. Riehm, *Messianic Prophecy*, tr. from German, 2nd ed., 1891, p. 133.

After we have considered these things we may raise the question of whether the prophecy has relevance also for us today: either through direct reference to the future in the way of prediction, or because it involves fundamental principles of divine truth, teaching that is eternally relevant regardless of time or place.

Let us look at a few illustrations of this Time-Dimension of the Present in relation to the message of the prophets. We shall not give a complete exegesis of each passage but rather present it in outline form, as an illustration and at the same time as a guide to further Bible study.

1. Take the preaching of Samuel. Though not one of the writing prophets in the sense of the men from Isaiah to Malachi his ministry is certainly significant for an understanding of prophecy. Samuel was a preacher who made known God's will in the concrete historical situation of which he was a part. We have two brief passages that seem to sum up his message to his people: I Samuel 12:19-25 (see especially verse 23) and I Samuel 15:22-23 (see also the context). Samuel is concerned with religious problems incident to the formation of the monarchy in Israel. The historical setting is that of the 11th century B.C. Predictive prophecy is present, but it is linked with the fundamental question of Israel's faithfulness or unfaithfulness to the Lord. "I will instruct you in the good and the right way.— Only fear the Lord, and serve him faithfully with all your heart.— To obey is better than sacrifice." There is a marked resemblance between the prophetic message of Samuel and the admonition of the psalmist:

> *Trust in the Lord, and do good;*
> *so you will dwell in the land, and enjoy security.*
> (Psalm 37:3)

Such preaching is equally relevant today, because our age is not essentially different from the age of Samuel; but we must not forget that it was to his own people in his own generation that the prophecy was spoken.

2. Take the book of Amos. The external situation is that of Assyrian imperialism and aggression in the 8th century B.C. The threat to Israel is indicated by the prophet in chapter 6:14, though the oppressor is not yet named. The internal situation is that of a smug prosperity, moral indifference, social corruption, and religious formalism, which makes the nation ripe for judgment. See by way of illustration Amos 2:6-8 and 5:21-23. Especially vivid is the picture of the deadening, destructive indifference of a prosperous secularism in chapter 6:4-7. To this situation Amos addresses himself as a prophet of God. What is his message? It is a "Woe" upon the existing evil situation in Israel (5:18; 6:1). There is a stern declaration of God's judgment (9:1-4). But there is also the urgent admonition to seek the Lord; to seek good and not evil, "that you may live" (5:4, 6, 14-15, 24). The situation was such as to call for repentance. Repentance might still avert the judgment, but the prophet does not say for sure that it will (5:15, "it may be"). If there be any message of hope it belongs to the remnant and to the future. One thing is sure: there can be no hope unless they seek the Lord and are willing to walk in His ways. How similar the preaching is to that of Samuel! How relevant also it is for our day, which is not essentially different from that of Amos. But it was to his own generation that Amos directed the words of his prophecy: he preached to a situation in Israel in the 8th century B.C.

3. The same is true of the contemporaries of Amos: Hosea in the north, Isaiah and Micah in the south. There are individual differences, but a marked similarity of situation is reflected in them all.

Take the book of Hosea. There is the same Assyrian background as in Amos, with this difference: the situation in Israel seems to be closer to 722 B.C. and the fall of Samaria. Something of the inner turmoil of that period can be seen in the message of the prophet. There is frequent mention of Assyria by name. The message is much the same: sin and impending judgment, with the hope of restoration on the horizon beyond the judgment because of the covenant faithfulness of God. We shall say more of that later. For the moment we are concerned with something else: the vivid awareness of the local scene on the part of the prophet, and the relevance of his message for his own generation. He was sent as a prophet to confront his own people in the latter part of the 8th century with a message from God that was meant in the first instance for them. If we understand its meaning for them we shall be in a better position to understand the relevance that it may have also for us.

Take the book of Isaiah, especially chapters 1-12. The general background of Assyrian aggression and invasion is the same as in Amos and Hosea, but in relation to Judah instead of Israel; and with a marked difference in political fortune at the moment. In chapter 1 there is a vivid picture of the Sennacherib invasion of 701 B.C. which swept to the very walls of Jerusalem. The reason for this judgment is the rebellion of God's people against their God.

> *Sons have I reared and brought up,*
> *but they have rebelled against me.*
> *The ox knows its owner,*
> *and the ass its master's crib;*
> *but Israel does not know,*
> *my people does not understand.* (1:2-3)

The nature of the judgment is a national affliction which leaves the country desolate.

> *Why will you still be smitten,*
> *that you continue to rebel?*
> *The whole head is sick,*
> *and the whole heart faint.* (1:5ff.)

The immediate outcome is the survival of "a very small remnant" (ASV).

> *If the Lord of hosts*
> *had not left us a few survivors,*
> *we should have been like Sodom,*
> *and become like Gomorrah.* (1:9)

The divine purpose, as interpreted by the prophet, is repentance, forgiveness, obedience, faithfulness, a renewed experience of the blessing of the covenant. See verses 16-17 and 18-20.

> *If you are willing and obedient,*
> *you shall eat the good of the land;*
> *but if you refuse and rebel,*
> *you shall be devoured by the sword;*
> *for the mouth of the Lord has spoken.*

A more thorough analysis of the chapter would confirm what G. A. Smith has said of it: "It is a clear, complete statement of the points which were at issue between the Lord and His own all the time Isaiah was the Lord's prophet."[28] It illustrates with special clarity what is true of other prophecies of Isaiah: he had a message that was meant first of all for his own people in his own generation. Other illustrations would be the Immanuel prophecy, so closely linked with the Syro-Ephraimite attempt to force Judah into a coalition against Assyrian aggression (chapter 7); the Davidic king prophecy in chapter 9:1-7, against the background of the darkness in chapter 8, a symbol of the Assyrian conquest; the anti-Assyrian prophecies of chapter 10; and the social and religious sins on which the prophet pronounces God's *Woe* in chapter 5. Even the beautiful hope passages seem to be in deliberate contrast with the darker situation that confronted the prophet. Whatever indications

---

[28] George Adam Smith, *The Book of Isaiah,* in the Expositor's Bible, vol. one, p. 4.

there may be of the touch of a later hand in some places, the prophecy of Isaiah as a whole is a part of contemporaneous history: it is directed to the historical situation of God's people in the 8th century B.C. If we understand what it meant for them *then* we shall be in a better position to understand what it may mean also for us *now*.

What we have said of Isaiah is true also of the book of Micah. There is the same Assyrian situation reflected, especially in chapters 1-3. The internal situation in Judah is morally, socially, and spiritually the same. There is the same historical realism in the expression of the prophet's hopes and fears. We sense as we read that this man too was a preacher sent by God with a message for his own day; and yet, there is at the same time a frightening resemblance to our own situation in our day. It is this similarity between *then* and *now* that makes the message relevant still.

4. Take the book of Nahum, which on internal grounds can be dated somewhere between 663 and 612 B.C. The theme is the imminent destruction of Nineveh, and with it the downfall of the Assyrian oppressor. What is said of Assyria may well apply to other oppressors at other times; but the prophet is speaking of the oppressor in his day. The message is a perfect illustration of what we mean by the element of historical contemporaneity in prophecy. A comparison with other prophetic passages which speak of Nineveh and Assyria will give further illustration of the same truth. The difference in viewpoint is interesting: Nahum predicts the destruction of Nineveh, which is seen as the bitter enemy of God and of His people; in Isaiah 10 the king of Assyria is seen as the rod of God's anger, which is used to discipline but not to destroy His people Israel; Hosea links Assyria with Egypt as the place of a new captivity for the people of Israel (9:3; 11:5, 11), in Jonah the preaching of judgment on Nineveh leads to repentance and to an experience of God's forgiving mercy; in Isaiah 19

Egypt and Assyria are given equal status with Israel as "a blessing in the midst of the earth, whom the Lord of hosts has blessed" (verses 24-25). Some of these prophecies project far beyond the day in which the prophets lived, but their initial point of attachment is the contemporaneous situation: they speak of a nation with which they were familiar, and not of some unknown nation in the future. Only as both Israel and Assyria can be seen to have a *representative* character will we understand its relevance also for us today.

5. Take the book of Habakkuk, which can be dated somewhere late in the 7th century B.C. The Assyrian empire has been replaced by the Chaldean, with no lessening of tensions for Judah. The internal situation in Judah is described in chapter 1:2-4; the problem posed by God's use of the Chaldeans "for chastisement" of Judah is set forth in chapter 1:5-17; in chapter 2:1-4 we have the solution of the problem; in chapter 2:5-19 the prophet pronounces Woe on the Chaldean sins, especially the sin of arrogant oppression; and in chapter 2:20 all the earth is admonished to keep silence before the Lord. Throughout the message we sense an awareness of the situation in which the prophet and his people were involved. We need to share that awareness if we are to understand the prophecy and to apply it to the situation in which we are involved.

6. Take the book of Jeremiah, the prophet whose personal experience is so closely tied in with the historical events of his day. The time of his ministry is indicated with unusual exactness (1:1-3). He is tremendously aware of the significance of the Chaldean threat to his people; and there is a spirit of personal tension because of his own role as a prophet of God in the current crisis. He predicts the Babylonian Captivity as something inevitable and points out the reasons for it; he proclaims the need of wholeheartedness in religion: a need then and now; he points out the basis for a hope of eventual

restoration. The inevitability of the Chaldean conquest of
Judah is a dominant note in his message, and he lived to see
the fulfilment of his prediction in the fall of Jerusalem, 587-
586 B.C. But more significant than the prediction of imminent
judgment, which occupies so large a part of his prophecies, is
the proclamation of "a new covenant" which God will make
with His people. The whole message is inseparably intertwined with contemporaneous history: it reflects the experiences and the events, the decisions and the decisive acts, the
hopes and the fears, of that critical period in sacred history
that we call *preexilic.* If we can see what it meant in terms
of God's people then we will begin to understand its relevance for us as the people of God today. We are not stretch-
ing the truth if we say that the historically contemporaneous
preaching of Jeremiah at this time of crisis in the history of
God's covenant people becomes decisive for the future understanding and interpretation of Biblical religion. The crashing
of false hopes is used by the Lord to provide the background
for the proclamation of the hope of a new covenant which will
fulfil the old.

7. Take the book of Ezekiel, the slightly younger contem-
porary and successor of Jeremiah. Most of Jeremiah's ministry
lay before the fall of Jerusalem in 587-586 B.C.; the ministry
of Ezekiel is divided about equally before and after this
crucial date. Jeremiah's ministry was performed in Jerusalem,
Ezekiel's in exile: but with keen awareness of the situation
"back home." There is in the book of Ezekiel something of
the same careful attention to dating that we see in the book
of Jeremiah. Ezekiel is no "carbon copy" of Jeremiah, and yet
there is a striking resemblance between the two in much of
their preaching. The analysis of the historical situation leading
up to the captivity is essentially the same. Both predict the
inevitability of the captivity. Both look beyond the judgment
to a "new thing" which the Lord will do: a restoration and a

renewal of the covenant relationship, which becomes also its fulfilment. Of this we shall say more later. Our concern now is to point up the close association between prophecy and history: history is reflected in prophecy, and prophecy interprets history. That is true of the book of Ezekiel, where there is a very understandable difference in tone between prophecies before and prophecies after the fall of Jerusalem.

8. Take the book of Haggai, which consists of four short prophecies dated in the same year and dealing with the same theme. The date is 520 B.C. The theme is the rebuilding of the temple. The whole outlook of the book is *postexilic*. The mission and the message of the prophet relate to an urgent present need. Our interpretation must begin with the pressing problem that confronted Haggai in the year 520. Only so can we safely look for a possible future relevance as well.

9. Take the book of Joel. Here the milieu within which the prophecy moves is not that of political history but that of a national calamity of a different sort: an unprecedented locust plague, which seems to forebode the coming of the day of the Lord (2:1). The word of God through the prophet is colored by the concrete event which confronted him. The immediate religious relevance of his message can be seen especially in chapter 2:12-14:

> "Yet even now," says the Lord,
>   "return to me with all your heart,
> with fasting, with weeping, and with mourning;
>   and rend your hearts and not your garments."
> Return to the Lord, your God,
>   for he is gracious and merciful,
> slow to anger, and abounding in steadfast love,
>   and repents of evil.
> Who knows whether he will not turn and repent,
>   and leave a blessing behind him,
> a cereal offering and a drink offering
>   for the Lord, your God?

It is easy to see the continuing relevance of such a message for God's people in any age, our own included; even as it is easy to see how it could become the starting point for a broader prophetic hope that projects far into the future. Nevertheless its initial significance is as a message for the concrete situation in the prophet's own day.

10. Take Isaiah 40-66. On the face of it we seem to hear words of comfort spoken to a people in captivity in Babylon. The reference to Cyrus, and to Babylon, and to the Chaldeans, are too specific to be interpreted in terms of poetic imagery. The promise of redemption and the hope of return from captivity must be understood first of all in terms of the historical and spiritual experience of Israel as the covenant nation of God. It is to Israel in Babylonian Captivity that the prophetic word in chapter 43:18-21 is first directed:

> *Remember not the former things,*
>   *nor consider the things of old.*
> *Behold, I am doing a new thing;*
>   *now it springs forth, do you not perceive it?*
> *I will make a way in the wilderness,*
>   *and rivers in the desert.*
> *The wild beasts will honor me,*
>   *the jackals and the ostriches;*
> *for I give water in the wilderness,*
>   *rivers in the desert,*
> *to give drink to my chosen people,*
>   *the people whom I formed for myself,*
> *that they might declare my praise.*

To recognize the relevance of the message for Israel in captivity is not to imply that its relevance is limited to them. The profound spiritual depths of the prophecy were not exhausted in the return from Babylon, though this return was a wonderful part of the fulfilment of the prophecy. There is a continuing and even an unfolding relevance which is clarified by later redemptive history. What the prophet foretold did not all come to pass as a result of the decree of Cyrus; but Cyrus was the Lord's anointed (45:1) to bring about a significant historical redemption which had deep and lasting significance in relation to the total redemptive plan of God. The prophets may be lifting their eyes to far distant horizons, but they do so from the vantage point of the position in time which God has given to them. Insofar as possible we who read their message today should try to take our stand with them where they stood, and to see the promised redemption as they saw it; then we shall be the better able to understand the New Testament claim to a fulfilment in Christ as the Redeemer of the world.

Historical contemporaneity—the Time-Dimension of the Present—is clearly evident in most Old Testament prophecies, in the great majority of the prophetic books. The permanently relevant teachings are also evident: concerning sin and judgment, concerning God's justice but also concerning His steadfast love, concerning His righteousness both in judgment and in redemption, concerning His forgiving mercy as the basis of the hope of salvation. The plea for repentance and for a wholehearted return to the Lord in faith and faithfulness lies at the very heart of the preaching. With such an understanding of the nature and purpose of prophecy we can readily see how relevant much of it is for the age in which we live: relevant because God remains the same, and because the human situation also is not greatly different.

II. The Time-Dimension of the Past

Let us consider next what we may call the Time-Dimension of the *Past*. That means specifically the early history of Israel, to which belongs their election to be in a peculiar sense the people of God. Prophetic preaching must be understood against the background of the covenant promise and hope, or within the covenant relationship. For the prophets preach to a people called into covenant with God and they reflect the covenant purpose and goal in their preaching. That includes the claims of the covenant upon Israel.

The two key passages in covenant history and religion are Genesis 12:1-3 and Exodus 19:3-6.

The first passage, though it does not use the term *berith* or covenant, indicates the basic terms of the covenant with Abraham: its contents, its promises, its demands, its expected response, its ultimate purpose. The climax is reached in the call of Abraham to be a blessing, or a channel of blessing, to all men. Chapter 17 clarifies the nature of the covenant as one of religious relationship: the phrase "their God" implies the corollary phrase that is so prominent in the Old Testament, "my people." Abraham and his seed are enjoined to keep the covenant not only by observing the sign of circumcision, but by a walk before God in the obedience of faith (17:1).

The second passage gives the basic terms of the covenant as reaffirmed or renewed in the Sinai-berith with Israel, Abraham's seed. It states the call of Israel to be God's *segullah*, or His very own, His priceless treasure; on condition, however, of obedience to the covenant, and with the declared purpose that they should be "a kingdom of priests and a holy nation" unto God.

In both passages there is indicated a close bond between three significant elements in Old Testament religion: the concepts of divine election, and of covenant, and of mission. In both passages there is envisioned a mutual faithfulness to the covenant on the part of God who initiates it in grace, and on the part of man who consents to it in faith.

It is within the framework of this covenant relationship that we must interpret the message of the prophets. Before we seek to confirm this assertion by means of illustration let us note a few things that are implied by the assertion. It implies:

1st, The covenant fellowship: that is, the relationship of "your God" and "my people"; the assurance of the presence of God, or the truth of Immanuel, God with us; the promise of spiritual blessings within the covenant experience.

2nd, The covenant theology: the significance of God's *hesed,* or steadfast love; of His *'emeth,* or truth and faithfulness; of His *tsedeq,* or righteousness; of His *yesha',* or salvation. These are keywords in Biblical religion, and therefore also in the theology of the prophets.

3rd, The covenant loyalty: the loyalty of God's people to their God, not as a matter of legal compulsion, but as a response in the obedience of faith. See Deuteronomy 10:12-13.

4th, The covenant Torah, or law: given for guidance in the good and the right way, with the experience of God's redeeming grace in the Exodus motivating His people to love and to keep His commandments. See Exodus 20, and compare Luther's Small Catechism, Part I.[29]

5th, The covenant purpose: the call of Israel to be a missionary people, a servant of God in relation to the rest of the world.

6th, The covenant goal: redemptive history moving towards the consummation of the covenant in a more glorious experience belonging to the Time-Dimension of the *Future.*

Let us look at a few illustrations of this Time-Dimension of the Past in relation to the message of the prophets. We shall group the illustrations topically instead of by books; for the dating of the prophecies is of less importance here than in relation to historical contemporaneity. The fundamental

---

[29] Martin Luther, *Small Catechism.* The explanation of each commandment begins with the words, "We should fear and love God so that . . ."

covenant doctrine does not vary much from one prophet to another, even though there are differences in emphasis. Where we meet new insights they are such as are implicit in the covenant from the beginning. That is true even when the prophet Jeremiah speaks of a "new covenant" which the Lord will make; for the newness does not consist in the terms of the covenant but in their successful realization.

1. Our first illustration concerns the positive commandments of God to His people. That involves what we call the Torah, or the law of God.

It is important that we have a right understanding of the Old Testament concept of Torah. A definition or two may help. One definition is that of "an authoritative rule of conduct whether revealed from within or from without" (Westminster Dictionary of the Bible).[30] "The law," says John D. Davis, "presents the commandments and claims of Jehovah to man."[31] According to R. B. Girdlestone, "The law of God is that which points out or indicates His will to man. It is not an arbitrary rule, still less is it a subjective impulse; it is rather to be regarded as a course of guidance from above."[32] "The law," says A. B. Davidson, "was given to the people in covenant. It was a rule of life, not of justification; it was guide to the man who was already right in God's esteem in virtue of his general attitude towards the covenant. The law is not to Israel a law of morals on the bare ground of human duty, apart from God's exhibition of His grace. It is a line marked out along which the life of the people or the person in covenant with God, and already right with God on that ground, is to unfold itself."[33] The law was not a prerequisite to be fulfilled before the making of the covenant: it was a response

---

[30] *The Westminster Dictionary of the Bible,* 1944.
[31] John D. Davis, *A Dictionary of the Bible,* 4th ed., 1924.
[32] R. B. Girdlestone, *The Synonyms of the Old Testament,* 1897, reprint 1948.
[33] A. B. Davidson, *The Theology of the Old Testament,* 1904, pp. 280-281.

in obedience to the covenant. For, as Geerhardus Vos says, "The law was given after the redemption from Egypt had been accomplished, and the people had already entered upon the enjoyment of many of the blessings of the berith."[34] W. A. Whitehouse distinguishes *Torah* from the Greek *nomos*, with which it is translated in the Septuagint, and sums up the meaning of Torah in this way; "Torah denotes the guidance or instruction which comes from God—it is the whole content of God's revelation of His nature and purpose, which incidentally makes clear man's responsibility before God."[35]

The sequence of events in the book of Exodus is significant. First comes the exodus redemption, then the covenant. See Exodus 19:3-6. The redemptive experience becomes the motivation to obedience to the Torah, the law of the covenant. See Exodus 20:1-2. We think now especially of the *moral* law as expressed, for example, in the Decalog. Compare the preamble to the Ten Commandments in Exodus 20 with Paul's words in Romans 12:1-2. In both instances the experience of God's redeeming grace and mercy is the motivation for a walk in the newness of life. According to Paul, the experience of saving grace is the only sufficient motivation for Christian ethics. It is not essentially different in the Old Testament, if the Torah is seen in its true relation to the covenant and to the redemption from Egypt in fulfilment of the covenant promise to Abraham.

We are concerned now with the *positive* requirements of the Torah and of the teaching of the prophets *within this covenant framework.*

Twice in the Old Testament we meet the question, "What does the Lord require of you?" and in each case the answer is given in terms that remind of covenant theology. The first is

---

[34] Geerhardus, Vos, *Biblical Theology*, 1948, p. 142.
[35] W. A. Whitehouse, in Richardson's *A Theological Word Book of the Bible*, 1952, art. "Law."

our English Bibles has the root meaning of "missing the mark." It is the failure to measure up to what we ought to be and by God's grace could be. The failure may be intentional or unintentional; but what difference does that really make if in either case the end is failure? Sin is shortcoming; it means to come short of the glory of God for which we were destined by creation, and yet more so, by the covenant of redemption. We come short of the character and the conduct that befits the people of God, those whom He has called into covenant with Himself.

2) The Hebrew word which is usually translated as *transgression* is *pesha.'* Its root meaning is really rebellion. We have a good instance of the use of the verb in Isaiah 1:2, "they have rebelled against me." The noun also implies a rebellion against a person who has rightful authority over you. It is a wilful revolt against God and against His Torah, with its requirements for the life of His people. There can be rebellion against God apart from covenant, the rebellion of creature against Creator; and the word is used of the sins of nations other than Israel. Perhaps we should say that there is something of a covenant relationship implied in the very creation of man. It is within the covenant of redemption, however, that we see this rebellion in its true light; for then it becomes a revolt not only against divine authority, but against divine love. May we speak of a covenant of redemption in the Old Testament? We certainly may if with the New Testament we see a fulfilment of the covenant of blessing with Abraham in Christ. If that be true, then the covenant with Israel, Abraham's seed, must also be interpreted as a part of redemptive history. It is within this framework of the covenant that the prophetic teaching concerning sin becomes pointedly relevant also for the New Testament Church.

c. We take as the third facet of our illustration some of the ways in which sin is described in the prophets. There are varying individual viewpoints of the same basic reality. In Jeremiah the sin of Israel is often called *backsliding* (see Jeremiah 8:5). In Hosea it is called harlotry (5:4) and lack of knowledge of the Lord (in the experiential sense of acknowledgement, 4:1, 5:4). In Isaiah sin is seen as preeminently pride and vanity (2:6-22). In Amos and Micah, but also in Isaiah, and elsewhere, the sin of injustice and oppression is singled out for special mention. Many of the prophets deplore a ritual religion without ethical content. One of the most telling indictments is the simple statement in Hosea 2:13, "[they] forgot me, says the Lord." Through them all runs the concept of a breach of covenant: either in relation to God Himself, so that He is not given the fear and love and trust which rightfully belong to Him (see the book of Deuteronomy); or in relation to men, in that God's good and righteous will for human conduct or social behavior is ignored and despised.

d. We take as the fourth facet of our illustration a few classic passages concerning sin as the prophets describe it and pronounce God's judgment upon it. We shall simply list them; for even a short thematic summary of each would become too lengthy for our purpose. A careful reading should be sufficient to show the reason for their selection to illustrate the point that we have made: that the prophetic message about sin must be understood within the framework of the covenant if we are to feel its full impact on the situation to which they addressed themselves, and its continuing relevance for the situation in which we find ourselves as the people of God under the new covenant.

Hosea 2:2-13; 4:1-6; 9:10.
Amos 1-2; 4:1; 8:4-6.
Isaiah 2:6ff.; 5:1-23; 59:1-15.
Micah 2:1-2; 3:1-4; 6:9ff.
Jeremiah 7.
Ezekiel 16 (especially verse 49).

3. Our third illustration concerns the nature of God, as seen in relation to the covenant and to Israel's unfaithfulness.

We might list here, and perhaps ought to discuss, the six covenant-related words in Psalm 40:10-11, for they are found also in the prophetic vocabulary. See the author's "The Psalms," especially the first essay, on "The God of the Covenant Revealed in Worship."[37] The God of the psalmist and of the prophets is a God of righteousness (RSV, saving help), of faithfulness, of salvation, of lovingkindness (RSV, steadfast love), of truth (RSV, faithfulness), and of tender mercies (RSV, mercy). Each phrase is pregnant with "covenant theology," in terms both of the nature and the activity of God. The primary emphasis is on the acts of God; and we shall not understand these acts apart from the covenant which He has made and to which He is faithful not only in word but in deed.

With Edmond Jacob we could outline the theology of the prophets, and of the whole Old Testament, under the two themes of the *presence* and the *acts* of God.[38] Then some of the words listed above become sub-divisions under the main themes.

We choose, however, a slightly different sequence. We shall mention without much comment seven things that seem fundamental to the prophetic message of God as the God of covenant with Abraham and with Israel. The continuing relevance of the message *for us* through its consummation in Jesus Christ, in whom we see "the light of the knowledge of the glory of God" (II Corinthians 4:6), we learn from the witness of the New Testament. For what is said in the Old Testament about the *hesed* and the *'emeth*, the mercy and the truth, the steadfast love and the faithfulness, of God receives its final and full expression when "the Word became flesh and dwelt among us, full of grace and truth" (John 1:14).

---

[37] John P. Milton, *The Psalms*, 1954, pp. 3-22.
[38] Edmond Jacob, *Theology of the Old Testament*, 1958.

The seven points in the prophetic message as it concerns the God of the covenant are these:

1st, That He is a God of justice, whose judgment in human situations is always impartial and just, without respect to persons. The classic example is in Amos 3:1-2. To the question of Abraham, "Shall not the Judge of all the earth do right?" (Genesis 18:25), the prophets would give unanimous answer, "Yes, of course! He is the God of justice, the God of just judgment."

2nd, That He is a God of steadfast love; a love so deep, so different from fickle human love, that it cannot bear the thought of letting His people go. The classic example is in Hosea 11:8-9; but these verses should be read in the context of the chapter, and indeed of the whole book.

3rd, That He is a God of faithfulness in spite of the faithlessness of His people. He seeks the erring and the rebellious with an urgent call to return. The classic passage is in Ezekiel 18:30-32. See also the reassuring epilogue to the book of Micah (7:18-20).

4th, That He is a God whose purpose with His people is to chasten rather than to destroy, whose judgments are meant in love for the salvation of His people and the consummation of His covenant with them. That is the thread of thought that runs through Isaiah 40-66 with its interpretation of the meaning of the Babylonian Captivity. The classic passage is in Isaiah 40:1-2. See also chapter 54:7-8 (and context).

5th, That He is above all a Saviour and a Redeemer, who is ever ready to forgive His people when they earnestly and sincerely seek Him. The redemption motif is especially prominent in Isaiah 40-66, but it is present in prophecy generally. Classic passages are Isaiah 43:25, with its striking phrase, "for my own sake"; Hosea 11:8-9, with its dramatic assertion, "for I am God and not man—and I will not come to destroy"; and

Ezekiel 34:11ff., "Behold, I, I myself will search for my sheep, and will seek them out."

6th, That He is a God who is infinitely holy, "who inhabits eternity" (Isaiah 57:15) and who must *humble* Himself even to behold the heavens and the earth (see Psalms 113:6, ASV); and yet, He is willing to condescend to them that are lowly in helping grace and mercy. The classic passage is Isaiah 57:15-16. The same thought, however, is implicit in the assurance of *God's presence* with His people, and in the promise of Immanuel, God with us.

7th, That He is a God "who has announced from of old the things to come" (Isaiah 44:7); whose ultimate purpose with the covenant is definite, and whose promise of its consummation in days to come is sure. At this point the Time-Dimension of the Past and also of the Present, begins to blend with the Time-Dimension of the Future, of which we have yet to speak. The prophets are never concerned with the Past for its own sake, but rather with its relation to the Present and to the Future; for in their concept of history *the present moment* is unintelligible apart from the past, and meaningless apart from the future.

We could continue, but since our purpose is only to illustrate we may stop here. The God of the prophets is the God of the fathers, the covenant God of Abraham, the Holy One of Israel, "the everlasting God, the Creator of the ends of the earth" (Isaiah 40:28). For the God of creation and the God of covenant are One; and He is also the God of redemption. Therefore He says to Israel,

> *I am the Lord, your Holy One,*
> *the Creator of Israel, your King.* (Isaiah 43:15)

And again He says,

> *For I am the Lord your God,*
> *the Holy One of Israel, your Savior.* (Isaiah 43:3)

And the believing remnant replies,

> *For thou art our Father,*
>   *though Abraham does not know us*
>   *and Israel does not acknowledge us;*
> *thou, O Lord, art our Father,*
>   *our Redeemer from of old is thy name.* (Isaiah 63:16)

The relevance of all this for today depends on how we read the New Testament. If we believe that the God of Abraham is the same as the God and Father of our Lord Jesus Christ, then the covenant theology of the prophets becomes relevant indeed.

III. *The Time-Dimension of the Future*

Let us consider finally what we may call the Time-Dimension of the *Future*. We have referred to it already in connection with the covenant. Because the covenant in its very nature is forward-looking, there is a forward-looking aspect, an eschatological significance, also to prophecy, which is so closely related to the covenant. It lies in the nature of prophecy to point beyond the present moment to the goal presupposed by the covenant. The prophets predict the future; but they do so primarily as a proclamation of their faith in the eventual attainment of God's covenant goal. Because predictive prophecy is rooted in the very nature of the covenant, the mission of the prophets is not to determine times and seasons, nor to identify individuals and nations from far distant historical situations: it is their mission rather to declare the ultimate glorious victory of the kingdom of God.

For note what this future aspect of prophecy in terms of the covenant implies. It implies:

1st, That there is a time of covenant consummation coming. The key-passage in the New Testament interpretation is Acts

3:17-26. See especially verse 21 in some of the variant versions which shed light on its real meaning: "the time for establishing all that God spoke by the mouth of his holy prophets from of old" (RSV);[39] "the times of restoration of all things" (ASV),[40] "intill tiderna for alltings återställelse" (Swedish);[41] "the period of the great Restoration" (Moffatt).[42] There are abundant illustrations in the Old Testament of the correctness of the New Testament interpretation at this point.

2nd, That because God is active in redemptive history this history is moving towards a divinely appointed goal. The prophets picture that goal in terms of *the covenant fulfilled.* In speaking of this fulfilment they employ much of the "times-coloring" of their own age, with the emphasis in the actual fulfilment seen to be upon the "fundamentals" rather than upon the "times-coloring." In the conviction of the prophets the goal of the covenant becomes the goal of history.

3rd, That the fundamentals of the covenant are seen in an ever increasing spiritual light. This is naturally true when the new covenant replaces, or fulfils, the old; but something of the New Testament illumination at this point is anticipated in the prophets. See especially Jeremiah, Ezekiel, and Isaiah 40-66.

4th, That there runs a double motif through all of history, including its final chapter: the double motif of judgment and redemption.

5th, That the finale of history is conceived of in the prophetic message as "the day of earth's redemption"; for the last word of God is not judgment but salvation.

Let us look at a few illustrations of this Time-Dimension of the Future in relation to the message of the prophets. An exhaustive treatment is out of the question, for it would in-

---

[39] Revised Standard Version of the Bible.
[40] American Standard Version of the Bible.
[41] Bibeln, eller den Heliga Skrift, 1917.
[42] James Moffatt, *A New Translation of the Bible.*

volve too much of the material. There is a sense in which the prophetic message in its entirety has significance for the future. That is why Jesus could claim that He came to fulfil it. But we think now of prophetic passages with more obvious eschatological implications.

1. Take the simple statement with which Obadiah ends his prophecy: "the kingdom shall be the Lord's" (verse 21). The thought is present in one form or another in almost every prophetic book. It is involved in the judgments upon the nations. It is a significant element in the Messianic prophecy of Isaiah 9:1-7. The same is true of Zechariah 9:9-10. See also the "righteous Branch" prophecy of Jeremiah (23:5-6), and the prediction in Ezekiel 21:25-27.

2. Take Hosea's prophecy of the "remarriage" between God and His people in chapter 2:14-20. The language clearly suggests a restoration which is final and permanent, and which fulfils the original intent of the covenant with Israel. The steadfast love of God prevails in the end. The valley of Achor, or Troubling, is made into a door of hope; for discipline is seen as leading to repentance, and an answer of love by God's people to God's own persuasive love. Then comes the fulfilment of the covenant in perfect fellowship, and of the marriage which symbolizes the covenant, in perfect love. Towards this future goal of the covenant the hope of the prophet is directed. What matters it that even he could not see the fulness of what that hope would involve in the fulfilment through Jesus Christ? He had his eyes on the goal, even if dimly seen, as from a great distance. He had faith that the covenant of God would not come to nought.

3. Take the new covenant of Jeremiah (31:31-34). We repeat what we have said before that there was nothing really new about the terms of the covenant. What God promises to do He had sought to do all along since the time of Abraham. Even Paul admits that "the scripture, foreseeing that God

would justify the Gentiles by faith, preached the gospel beforehand to Abraham" (Gal. 3:8). It would be a gross injustice
to interpret the covenant with Abraham or the covenant with
Israel at Sinai as if utterly devoid of any concern for the religious quality that we call *inwardness*. The contrast in Jeremiah is not an absolute one; and yet, the new covenant is more
than a renewal of the old. It is indicative of fulfilment. God
will not let Israel's breaking of the covenant hinder Him from
keeping it, or from bringing His gracious purpose with the
covenant to fruition. He will not stop in His redemptive love
until He gains the heart response of His people, thus making
the fellowship promised in the covenant beautifully real. God
will make a new and supreme attempt to bring about a fulfilment of the covenant in actual experience, and He will not
fail. Even Jeremiah did not know all that this would require
of God in order to be accomplished. He speaks of forgiveness,
but not of redemption. The Cross of Christ is not in the fore-
ground of the prophecy where we might expect it. We still
need the gospel to clarify the prophecy. We need to know
the love of God in Christ to see the dynamic power that makes
the covenant new. It is only when the love of Christ controls
the hearts, and minds, and will of men that the original covenant with Abraham and his seed becomes new with the newness of fulfilment.

4. Take Ezekiel's prophecies about "a new heart" and "a
new spirit" in chapters 18:30-32 and 36:24-28. He too foresees
and foretells the coming of "a new thing"; and the viewpoint
fluctuates between a renewal of covenant, as in Hosea, and a
new covenant, as in Jeremiah. In either case the prophecy is
indicative of a future covenant fulfilment. The vision of the
Valley of Dry Bones in chapter 37 is a striking symbol of the
rebirth of the covenant nation; and in the closing paragraph
of the chapter there is an idyllic picture of a renewed covenant. Though the phraseology of the prophecy is borrowed

from the covenant with the fathers, the prophecy looks to the
future: it seems to envision a permanent realization of the
covenant in actual experience, an ideal fulfilment of what it
promised. If there be truth in the prophecy, it cannot be limited to a restoration from captivity, but must point beyond it
to "the new age." The same is true of the vision of the temple
and of "the new Jerusalem" in Ezekiel 40-48. The closing note
of the book is a confident reaffirmation of the central idea in
the covenant, the presence of the Lord with His people: "And
the name of the city henceforth shall be, The Lord is there"
(48:35). "Henceforth" suggests permanence. In the faith of
the prophet the goal of the covenant has been reached.

5. Take the prophecy about the creation of "new heavens
and a new earth" in Isaiah 65-66. The comprehensive nature
and the climactic position of the prophecy is unmistakable.
That whereof the prophet speaks is not a stop along the way
but the end. The chapters indicate not only a new creation
but a new covenant; for "the Creator of the ends of the earth"
(Isaiah 40:28) is "the Creator of Israel" (43:15).

> *For as the new heaven and the new earth*
>   *which I will make*
> *shall remain before me, says the Lord;*
>   *so shall your descendants and your name remain.*
> *From new moon to new moon,*
>   *and from sabbath to sabbath,*
> *all flesh shall come to worship before me,*
>   *says the Lord.* (66:22-23)

In the light of the New Testament it seems evident that the
Old Testament prophet, even if we must make allowance for
something of local coloring both in language and in thought-
forms, anticipated "the times of restoration of all things." In
the faith of the prophet the goal of history is reached in the
new creation, wherein the covenant of redemption is also fulfilled. "Behold, I make all things new." It remains for the New

Testament to clarify the central place of Christ in relation to this fulfilment. See II Corinthians 5:17; Romans 8:19ff.

We could continue almost indefinitely with illustrations of the eschatological significance of prophecy, the Time-Dimension of the Future. The frequent pictures of restoration, of redemption, of regeneration, of return from captivity, of covenant renewal, all combine something of this forward-looking aspect of prophecy with its relevance for the historically contemporaneous moment. If we take these frequent references that imply a final redemptive act of God and divest them of the local "times-coloring"; if we connect them with the typologically significant functions and the eschatologically significant promises of a king (who will fulfil the vocation of the house of David), a prophet (who will fulfil the prophetic vocation by speaking the last "word" that reveals God), a priest (after the order of Melchizedek, but who will fulfil the vocation of Israel to be a priest of God), a servant (who will fulfil the vocation of Israel as the servant of the Lord), a people (who will fulfil the calling of Israel to be a holy nation unto the Lord),—then we have in essence the prophetic message of hope which the New Testament confirms: a hope fulfilled in Christ, yet moving forward to the day of "the great Restoration" of which Christ is God's own guarantee for the faith of His people.

The Time-Dimension of prophecy: the Present always seen in the light of the Past, and the Future in the light of both! The theme of prophetic preaching: the ultimate coming of the kingdom of God in all its universal and spiritual implications, in fulfilment of the covenant of blessing with Abraham! The prophetic concept of history: the mighty acts of God, in terms of the judgment-redemption motif and within the framework of the covenant, moving towards a goal! The continuing significance of prophecy: the "clear continuity of theological principle," of which Hebert writes in "The

Throne of David," and which is reflected in the New Testament interpretation;[43] the "Auffrischung" of which Ed. Böhl speaks in his "Christologie des Alten Testaments" and which is also reflected in the New Testament usage.[44] "The prophets are appointed in order to preserve to the people of Israel the blessings already at hand, and ever anew to impress upon the people the right understanding of those blessings of salvation (Heilsguter). They are expositors (Ausleger), legitimized by God Himself, of the Word of God already present; something absolutely new we should not expect of them, but rather the renewing (Auffrischung) of the old."

Do you see the difference between such an understanding of prophecy and much current preaching of prophecy? Where is the rightful emphasis? It is on the heart and not on the periphery of the prophetic message; on religious fundamentals and not on speculative trivia in interpretation; on God's eternal covenant and on His kingdom rather than on the human foes that strut across the stage. It is what I believe to be the evangelical emphasis and in harmony with the New Testament interpretation.

At any rate we cannot preach prophecy as we should unless we know something about its threefold Time-Dimension: Past, Present, and Future.

---

[43] A. G. Hebert, *The Throne of David*, 1946, pp. 130-131.
[44] Ed. Böhl, *Christologie des Alten Testaments*, p. 182.

The Prophets as
Preachers of the
Whole Counsel of God

Introduction

May I first define our field of study more exactly and indicate the focal point of our theme.

When we speak of the prophets we mean now the writing prophets of the Old Testament, the Latter Prophets as distinguished from the Former Prophets of the Hebrew Canon. We shall not consider the historical books from Joshua to Kings, which are listed in the Hebrew Bible as prophetic books. We shall not consider Moses and David, who were men with prophetic endowment; though we in our thinking associate the one with the Law and the other with the Psalms. We shall pass by men like Elijah, Elisha, Nathan, and Gad; a few of the many true prophets whom we meet on the pages of the Old Testament Scriptures, but who wrote no books. In other words, we are not concerned here with the institution of prophetism as a whole, though our theme might well lead us that far eventually if we pursued it to the end. For our purpose we are limiting the field of study to the four books listed in the Hebrew Bible as Isaiah, Jeremiah, Ezekiel, and the Twelve: to the men who constitute the writing prophets from Isaiah to Malachi.

We want to think of these men as preachers. Before everything else they were just that. We may be sure that much of their preaching, like that of Paul in New Testament times, was an oral message, that was spoken to people who would listen *before* it was set down in written form to make its permanent appeal to them who would read. These men preached wherever folks gathered who could be preached to; in the streets and market-places as well as in the courts of kings; to individuals and small groups to whom God sent them, but also to the teeming populace of a Nineveh, and of a Samaria or a Jerusalem; with words, but also through signs and wonders, by which their spoken message was often supported and made more vivid: but through it all, it was real preaching to the hearts and consciences of men, a preaching with a definite spiritual purpose. Of course they also predicted the future, whenever God gave them that sort of a message to proclaim· but by a purely quantitative scale of comparison, they spent far more time in preaching righteousness than they did in foretelling the future. They were busy proclaiming, interpreting, and applying the will of God to their own generation. Or as our theme suggests, and as we propose to try to prove, they were preachers of the whole counsel of God.

This is the focal point in the theme before us: the prophets were preachers, and they preached the whole counsel of God. Is it perhaps a point too self-evident to need our feeble attempt to prove it? I would like to think so; but I am often quite startled by some of the misconceptions, even in my own Lutheran circles, concerning the everlasting spiritual verity and value of the prophetic message. There are some who make it simply an arsenal from which to draw at will ammunition for a decidedly exaggerated and explosively dangerous prediction of events still future, or belonging to the time of the end. There are some who make it merely the well from which to draw a muddied social gospel instead of the pure waters of salvation. There are still others who dismiss it with a careless indifference, as if the prophets were either antagonistic to the New Testament gospels and epistles or quite without spiritual value in comparison with them. We may indeed ask in all seriousness, "Is there a fundamental unity between the preaching of the prophets and of the apostles?" Are the basic truths of God's message eternally the same, even if it be conceded without debate that they may be more or less clearly proclaimed, and more or less clearly perceived? Can we rightfully speak of the prophets as being preachers of the whole counsel of God?

It seems to me that we can indeed truthfully speak of the prophets as preaching the whole counsel of God. Let me at least try to establish, or shall I say demonstrate, the point. And if we should end up with two or three essential qualifications of the thesis set forth in our theme, which may seem to be at variance with it? Let us take care of that as we come to it!

I. What is meant by the whole counsel of God?

We face then this question: What is meant by the whole counsel of God?

The phrase, as we well know, is Paul's. We find it in Acts 20:26-27, where in taking farewell of the Ephesian elders at Miletus Paul says to them: "Therefore I testify to you this day that I am innocent of the blood of all of you, for I did not shrink from declaring to you the whole counsel of God." It is evident that the words constitute a personal vindication by Paul of his preaching. He had been frank and fearless in that preaching. He had spoken everything that they needed to hear, and that God had given him to speak; and the message was not only such as to clear Paul of any responsibility or guilt for any sinner's death: it was so sufficient and complete that he dares to call it "the whole counsel of God."

What did Paul mean? What did he include under that whole counsel of God which he had preached?

It isn't exactly easy to answer. Paul himself does not tell us in so many words. We may be sure that he does not mean to imply that God had let him in on all His secrets, so that he knew as much as God knew. Even that remarkable word in the book of Amos,

> Surely the Lord God does nothing,
> without revealing his secret
> to his servants the prophets (3:7),

does not necessarily make the prophets all-knowing. But we may be just as sure that Paul did mean that he had preached everything that they needed to hear in order to be saved. Can we be more specific than that? Does the whole counsel of God include the full teaching of Paul as we have it in his epistles: the Christology of Colossians, the spiritual anthropology of the early chapters of Romans, the soteriology of Romans and Galatians, the ecclesiology of Ephesians, the eschatology of Thessalonians, the pastoral regulations of Timothy and Titus, the church discipline of Corinthians? If so, our task in defining this phrase from Acts 20 would be to prepare a compendium of Pauline doctrine, and our task in defending the theme before us would be to present a detailed comparison of this teaching with that of the Old Testament prophets.

I wonder, however, whether that is the right approach to the interpretation of Paul's words to the Ephesian elders! Is there not some safe and acceptable way of summing up this counsel of God, and of showing the main lines of its application to the situation at Ephesus and in every place?

It would seem that we have such a simplification of the essentials of the apostolic preaching in the context, in Paul's own words on this very occasion. Note the significant parallelism between verse 20 and verse 27: in verse 20 we read, "I did not shrink from declaring to you anything that was profitable," and in verse 27, "I did not shrink from declaring to you the whole counsel of God." There is an evident equation in Paul's mind between the whole counsel of God and that which was profitable. He is thinking in terms of that which profits the hearer, which is the purpose of the preaching. Then in verse 21 he states what may be called the very heart of preaching that is profitable to hear: "testifying both to Jews and to Greeks of repentance to God and of faith in our Lord Jesus Christ." The "profitable" preaching of Paul boiled down to this: repentance and faith, toward God and toward our Lord Jesus Christ, and the preaching of those truths that will bring about these results! The apostle adds nothing when he says in verse 24 that the aim of his ministry was "to testify to the gospel of the grace of God"; nor when he says in verse 31, that he "did not cease night or day to admonish every one with tears"; nor when he speaks in verse 32 of "the word of his grace, which is able to build you up and to give you the inheritance among all those who are sanctified." The preaching of repentance to God and of faith in our Lord Jesus Christ *is* the gospel of grace. Repentance to God and faith in Christ are the framework of the whole counsel of God as preached by Paul.

Don't be misled by the brevity and conciseness of Paul's summary. What it lacks in breadth and length it makes up for in depth. It includes: 1st, the preaching of God as the Scripture makes Him known, and of the holy will of God in relation to man; 2nd, the preaching of sin, or of man's transgression and even rebellion against this holy God, and of the need of repentance lest he perish in his sin; 3rd, the preaching of Christ as Saviour and Lord, even the truth of the Cross of Christ as the redemptive basis of saving grace; and 4th, the preaching of faith in Christ, or the experience of grace through the faith-appropriated forgiveness of sins. Other items are drawn into the orbit of these central constellations; such as the reference to inheritance in verse 32. The summary statement still stands: "testifying both to Jews and to Greeks of repentance to God and of faith in our Lord Jesus Christ."

Before we apply the test of this summary to the preaching of the prophets it may be well to note another such summary from the lips of Jesus himself: a summary based upon the teaching of the Old Testament Scriptures, including the prophets. The passage in question is in Luke 24:44-48. "These are my words which I spoke to you, while I was still with you, that everything written about me in the law of Moses and the prophets and the psalms must be fulfilled." Then he opened their minds to understand the scriptures, and said to them, "Thus it is written, that the Christ should suffer and on the third day rise from the dead, and that repentance and forgiveness of sins should be preached in his name to all nations, beginning from Jerusalem. You are witnesses of these things."

Once more there are four points in the summary: 1) the sufferings of Christ; 2) His resurrection; 3) repentance; and 4) the forgiveness of sins. The correspondence between the two statements, by Paul and by Jesus, is not lost on us, I trust. Both place the Christ of God in the center as the object of faith and worship; both stress the preaching of repentance which, whether so stated or not, must be to God; and the faith of the Pauline statement is the faith that leads to the remission of sins in Jesus' Name. Even the universality is alike; for Paul testified "both to Jews and to Greeks," and Jesus said that the preaching should be "to all nations, beginning from Jerusalem."

II. *Did the prophets preach the whole counsel of God?*

If we admit that we have in the two statements by Paul and by Jesus a true epitome of the whole counsel of God we are ready to apply the test to the prophets as preachers. Were they preachers of the whole counsel of God?

Let us not be too quick with our answer. The striking contrast in Hebrews 1:1-2 between God's speaking "by the prophets" and "by a Son" should give us pause; especially when we read it in Weymouth's translation: God spoke by the prophets "in many fragments."[45] It is to be admitted that each prophet may have had only a portion of the whole counsel of God in his part of the joint message. It is conceded also that with the coming of Jesus Christ, the Word of God Incarnate, the whole counsel of God may have taken on a clarity and completeness which it could not have in the prophetic message. There is a real progress in revelation between the Old Testament and the New. Of this we should be aware. But the distinction between the two is relative rather than absolute; it is one of degree, not of kind. There is no inconsistency between the two. Even Paul, who claimed to preach the whole counsel of God, confessed for himself and for all Christians, "For our knowledge is imperfect and our prophecy imperfect; but when the perfect comes, the imperfect will pass away. —For now we see in a mirror dimly, but then face to face. Now I know in part; then I shall understand fully, even as I have been fully understood" (I Cor. 13:9-10, 12). The whole counsel of God does not mean perfect and complete insight into the will and ways of God: it means the truth of God as revealed for purposes of salvation and sanctification, or unto the end of a truly spiritual life. This

---

[45] Richard Francis Weymouth, *The New Testament in Modern Speech,* 4th ed., 1924.

truth centers in the preaching of repentance toward God and of faith in our Lord Jesus Christ unto the remission of sins.

We have Christ's own word for it that the prophetic preaching, the Old Testament Scriptures, included these things. What a course in Old Testament exegesis he must have given Cleopas and his companion on the way to Emmaus! "And he said to them, 'O foolish men, and slow of heart to believe all that the prophets have spoken! Was it not necessary that the Christ should suffer these things and enter into his glory?' And beginning with Moses and all the prophets, he interpreted to them in all the scriptures the things concerning himself" (Luke 24:25-27). We wish that we might have sat in; that the whole conversation might have been recorded; that we had been given a Jesus-edited commentary on the whole of the Old Testament instead of His brief comment on a passage here and there. But it may be better that we have been left to discover for ourselves the full significance of Jesus' claim that "*everything* written about me—might be fulfilled" (Luke 24:44). It may be better that we let the Spirit of Christ *now* open our minds to understand the Scriptures; using the key which the Lord himself has given: "Thus it is written, that the Christ should suffer and on the third day rise from the dead, and that repentance and forgiveness of sins should be preached in his name to all nations, beginning from Jerusalem" (Luke 24:46, 47). It may be better for this reason among others, that it seems to be a law of the Kingdom of God that only he who seeks shall find. Truth that is set too openly or easily before a man often seems to possess little interest or value for him. We may be sure that our Lord Jesus Christ knew what He was doing when He summed up His exegesis in a few lines and left us to discover the rest; when He gave us a key and told us to use it; and when He left this sufficient promise in connection with the coming of the Holy Spirit, the Spirit of truth, "he will guide you into all the truth" (John 16:13).

We want to use the key now on that portion of Scripture which we call the prophets.

A. Concerning God

If we had only the prophetic books of the Bible before us, would we have a true knowledge of God? What is God like according to the prophets? Do they have an adequate theology, or must we borrow from other sources to complete it?

We shall not stop for many proof passages, however profitable that might be. It would take too long to exhaust the list. We would dare to suppose that you know something of the spirit and of the message of these men whom we call the prophets. We would invite each one to that intimate and familiar friendship with the prophets as men and as ministers of God which comes only through faithful reading of the books they have written. For from such an acquaintance with them will come the conviction that the God of the prophets is not only the God of the fathers, the God of Abraham, and of Isaac, and of Jacob, but that He is the same as the God and Father of our Lord Jesus Christ. (See Eph. 1:3 for the terminology used there.)

A few illustrations are in order.

He is first and foremost according to the prophets "the living God." Hosea speaks of the day when it shall again be said of Israel that they are "Sons of the living God" (1:10). So also Jeremiah asserts:

> But the Lord is the true God;
> he is the living God and the everlasting King. (10:10)

The usual formula of the oath, "As the Lord lives" (Jer. 4:2), or, if God is the speaker, "As I live, says the Lord" (Isaiah

49:18), bears witness to this faith in the living God. The
God of the prophets is "God in truth" (see ASV mg., Jer.
10:10). He *is* God, and is not merely called God. As the living
God He enters actively into the affairs of men, in judgment
and in salvation, with acts of sustenance and of governance.
God lives!

He is also the only God. The prophets are thoroughgoing
monotheists, even if they sometimes accommodate their language to those who believe otherwise, and therefore speak
comparatively of "other gods." It is in the latter part of the
book of Isaiah that we find the clearest declarations of the
uniqueness of the Lord, the King of Israel and his Redeemer,
the Lord of hosts:

> *They have no knowledge*
> *who carry about their wooden idols,*
> *and keep on praying to a god*
> *that cannot save.*
> *Declare and present your case;*
> *let them take counsel together!*
> *Who told this long ago?*
> *Who declared it of old?*
> *Was it not I, the Lord?*
> *And there is no other god besides me,*
> *a righteous God and a Savior;*
> *there is none besides me.*
> *Turn to me and be saved,*
> *all the ends of the earth!*
> *For I am God, and there is no other.* (Isaiah 45:20-22)

This goes beyond the commandment, "You shall have no other
gods before (or besides) me" (Exod. 20:3). This is the witness to the truth that constituted the cornerstone of the
prophetic faith: Yahwe alone is God. Yahwe alone lives. In
this confession of faith all the prophets concur. It was the
faith which undergirded their preaching at all times, even
when it did not find formal expression as in a creed.

The prophets also preached a personal God, whose relationship to men is that of one personality to another—an "I -thou" relationship. He is as a husband to Israel (Hos. 2:16; Isa. 54:5; Jer. 31:32), and as a father (Hos. 11:1; Isa. 63:16). He is our Maker and our Redeemer (Isa. 54:5). He is a God who is described in the human terms of seeing, hearing, smelling, tasting, speaking, determining, remembering, repenting; because these terms, even if we admit that they are anthropomorphic in character and therefore inadequate to describe the essential nature of God who is Spirit, convey to us the impression of a personal Being, and such God is. He is preached by the prophets as One who has the qualities or attributes of personality, a Person. Never is He equated with force, or with natural laws, or with the sum total of things in the universe. He is always above them, apart from them, and yet author of them, and actively operative in them. He is ever the transcendent as well as immanent personal God. How tenderly intimate the personal relationship of this God with man can be according to the prophets! It seems that almost every term applied to Christ in the gospels, or by Christ applied to His Father in heaven, is in the prophetic preaching applied to the God of Abraham, who is also the God of His people Israel: such terms as Maker, Creator, Redeemer, Savior, husband, Father, Lord. They that seek Him shall live (Amos 5:4). It is He who like a father teaches His children to walk (Hos. 11:3-4), and carries them in His arms (Hos. 11:3; Isa. 40:11). He pleads with the erring and sinning to return (Isa. 55:6-9; Ezek. 18:23, 30-32). His heart rebels at the very thought of giving them up (Hos. 11:8-9).

The God of prophetic preaching is the Almighty Maker of heaven and earth, who is at the same time the covenant God of Israel and the God of the whole earth (Isa. 54:5). He is the Creator of the ends of the earth (Isa. 40:28) and He is the Creator of Israel (Isa. 43:15). Another way of putting it is to say that He is both the God of creation and the God of history; and His omnipotent power is manifest in both creation and history. The classic chapter that bears witness to this truth is Isaiah 40. The language is vivid and bold:

> *Who has measured the waters in the hollow of his hand*
> *and marked off the heavens with a span,*
> *enclosed the dust of the earth in a measure*
> *and weighed the mountains in scales*
> *and the hills in a balance?* (40:12)

> *Behold, the nations are like a drop from a bucket,*
> *and are accounted as the dust on the scales;*
> *behold, he takes up the isles like fine dust.* (40:15)

According to Micah, when the Lord enters into judgment it is as if He comes forth from His place to tread with giant steps "upon the high places of the earth" (1:3). It is this same awesome majesty and might of the Lord that becomes the reassuring comfort of His people when in affliction. That is the wonderful closing note in the 40th chapter of Isaiah.

> *Why do you say, O Jacob,*
> *and speak, O Israel,*
> *"My way is hid from the Lord,*
> *and my right is disregarded by my God"?*
> *Have you not known? Have you not heard?*
> *The Lord is the everlasting God,*
> *the Creator of the ends of the earth.*
> *He does not faint or grow weary,*
> *his understanding is unsearchable.*
> *He gives power to the faint,*
> *and to him who has no might he increases strength.*
> (40:27-29)

What is more, every fundamental attribute of God as set forth by systematic theology is ascribed to Him somewhere in the prophets; and these attributes shine through incessantly even where they are not formally stated. We cite a few of them: God is spiritual (Isa. 40), eternal (Isa. 57:15), unchangeable (Mal. 3:6), everywhere present (Amos 9), almighty (Ezek. 1:24), all-knowing (Zech. 4:10b), all-wise (Isa. 40:13), holy (Isa. 6:3; see the whole book, especially the emphasis on the Holy One of Israel), righteous (Jer. 23:6; see also the book of Amos with its strong emphasis on righteousness among men as a divine requirement), faithful and true (Isa. 49:7), good (Jer. 33:11), gracious and merciful (Joel 2:13; Jonah 4:2), compassionate (Micah 7:19), who "in his love and in his pity" redeems men (Isa. 63:9) and becomes their Savior (Isa. 63:8). Even the Triuneness of God, though not a specific subject of revelation, seems at times to be reflected in the prophetic preaching. Isaiah like David speaks of "his holy Spirit" (Isa. 63:10). Whatever difference there may be in theological insight his words, "But they rebelled and grieved his holy Spirit," stand on the same religious plane as the Pauline injunction, "And do not grieve the Holy Spirit of God" (Eph. 4:30). And we might seriously ask whether the person whom we call "the Servant of the Lord" (Hebrew *'eved*, Greek *pais*) is not as much a son as a servant; for he seems to fulfil the vocation of Israel which was both that of servant and son (see Exod. 4:22-23, and later references to these two aspects of Israel's vocation). Be that as it may, it is evident from the similarity of the prophetic language in speaking of God as Savior to that of the apostles when they speak of Christ the Son as the Savior, that the full truth of revelation concerning the Son of God as the Savior of the world is just beyond the horizon; with enough light already coming over the horizon's edge to foretell the dawn, and to direct the hearts of men in true faith *to God their Savior.*

B. Concerning Christ

What then shall we say of the prophetic preaching and Christ? Did they know Christ? Did they preach Him?

Suppose we let Jesus himself have the word first. On this point of exegesis we know what His interpretation was. He said that the prophets *did* testify of Him; just as He said of Abraham, the man who believed the Lord and had his faith reckoned to him as righteousness (Gen. 15:6), "Your father Abraham rejoiced that he was to see my day; he saw it and was glad" (John 8:56). No merely human interpreter would dare to speak in that way. We dare to say it now only by the authority of Christ. His authority confirms the truth of those foreshadowings of His coming which we find in the prophets themselves. They did see Christ. They saw Him by faith. They saw Him dimly as one still far off. They saw the promise of Him in the saving acts of God in their own day. The Christ was present in the divine purpose revealed by those saving acts. While it was not given them to see as we see the personal relationship between God the Savior and this Messianic servant whom He would send to do His will and to accomplish His work (see John 4:34); while they did not possess the theological insight of Paul, which is based on the finished redemptive work of Christ; while they lacked the sort of knowledge that we have of the historical Jesus Christ; while we would not want to subtract one iota from Jesus' words of promise concerning the work of the Holy Spirit as the Spirit of truth, "he will guide you into all the truth" (John 16:13): we can nevertheless say that the prophets had and preached the whole counsel of God. God the Savior was in their preaching: the Savior God who is constantly turning earthward with thoughts and acts of redemption, and whose salvation comes finally to its full fruition in Christ the Son, the Savior of the world. Salvation was in their preaching:

faith in God as their Savior and Redeemer, and something of hope in respect to a salvation to come through one whom God would send.

How much of faith and hope in such a coming one; and how much of knowledge concerning the Savior to come? How much did the prophets know and preach about the nature of His coming and of His person and of His work?

An exhaustive treatment is out of the question here. We can only indicate a few of the main lines along which the thoughts and the hopes of the prophets were directed by the Spirit of God.

We may say in general that the prophetic preaching concerning the Messiah attaches itself to the promise given to David, "Moreover the Lord declares to you that the Lord will make you a house." (See II Sam. 7:11b, in the context of the whole chapter.) We might be inclined to ask whether the Lord really intended this to be a promise with Messianic significance. I believe that He did. Certainly David came to understand it so. But for our purpose here it is sufficient to show that the prophets understood it so, and that they spoke of the salvation to come as if linked in some close way with the son of David. For example:

> There shall come forth a shoot from the stump of Jesse,
>   and a branch shall grow out of his roots.
> And the Spirit of the Lord shall rest upon him,
>   the spirit of wisdom and understanding,
>   the spirit of counsel and might,
>   the spirit of knowledge and the fear of the Lord.
> And his delight shall be in the fear of the Lord.
>   (Isaiah 11:1-3)

"In that day the root of Jesse shall stand as an ensign to the peoples; him shall the nations seek, and his dwellings shall be glorious" (Isa. 11:10).

For to us a child is born,
  to us a son is given;
and the government will be upon his shoulder,
  and his name will be called
"Wonderful Counsellor, Mighty God,
  Everlasting Father, Prince of Peace."
Of the increase of his government and of peace
  there will be no end,
upon the throne of David, and over his kingdom,
  to establish it, and to uphold it
with justice and with righteousness
  from this time forth and for evermore. (Isaiah 9:6-7)

"Behold, the days are coming, says the Lord, when I will raise up for David a righteous Branch, and he shall reign as king and deal wisely, and shall execute justice and righteousness in the land. In his days Judah will be saved, and Israel will dwell securely. And this is the name by which he will be called: 'The Lord is our righteousness'" (Jer. 23:5-6).

"And I will set up over them one shepherd, my servant David, and he shall feed them: he shall feed them and be their shepherd. And I, the Lord, will be their God, and my servant David shall be prince among them; I, the Lord, have spoken" (Ezek. 34:23-24).

"Afterward the children of Israel shall return and seek the Lord their God, and David their king; and they shall come in fear to the Lord and to his goodness in the latter days" (Hos. 3:5).

In that day I will raise up
  the booth of David that is fallen
and repair its breeches,
  and raise up its ruins,
  and rebuild it as in the days of old;
that they may possess the remnant of Edom
  and all the nations who are called by my name,
  says the Lord who does this. (Amos 9:11-12; see Acts 15)

But you, O Bethlehem Ephrathah,
  who are little to be among the clans of Judah,
from you shall come forth for me
  one who is to be ruler in Israel,
whose origin is from of old,
  from ancient days.
Therefore he shall give them up until the time
  when she who is in travail has brought forth;
then the rest of his brethren shall return
  to the people of Israel.
And he shall stand and feed his flock in the strength of the Lord,
  in the majesty of the name of the Lord his God.
And they shall dwell secure, for now he shall be great
  to the ends of the earth. (Micah 5:2-4)

Rejoice greatly, O daughter of Zion!
  Shout aloud, O daughter of Jerusalem!
Lo, your king comes to you;
  triumphant and victorious is he,
humble and riding on an ass,
  on a colt the foal of an ass.
I will cut off the chariot from Ephraim
  and the war horse from Jerusalem;
and the battle bow shall be cut off,
  and he shall command peace to the nations;
his dominion shall be from sea to sea,
  and from the River to the ends of the earth.
                                    (Zechariah 9:9-10)

There are many others; less specific, but nevertheless indicative of how prophetic preaching centered the future hope
in the promise to David. The promise symbolized dominion
and victory, the coming of the rule of God through His
anointed king, the establishment of the kingdom of God on
earth. When Jesus on one memorable occasion asked the
question, "What do you think of the Christ? Whose son is
he?" they answered without hesitation, "The son of David"
(Matt. 22:42). And so far they were right. Where they had
failed to think through was with respect to the real nature of

His kingship and of His relationship as the son of David to God.

Had the prophets thought through at this point? Were they in the clear about these things? We must admit that they had not reached the clarity of the New Testament teaching concerning either the nature of the kingdom or the person of the king. That is not strange; nor does it contradict our thesis that they were preachers of the whole counsel of God. The prophets spoke of the coming deliverer in terms of His work rather than of His person. It is significant that even David, the prototype of the Messianic king, thought of himself *as the servant* of the Lord. (See II Samuel 7, where the original promise to David is recorded.) When we begin to examine the nature of the service ascribed to the anointed king we can see how close the prophets come to Jesus' own concept of the kingship. In speaking of His salvation they often describe a work which only God could perform. They saw the Messiah as one sent by God, and His work as God's work; so that the full truth of the Oneness of Him who sends with Him who is sent seems to tremble on the brink of open revelation. They would have understood what Jesus meant when He said, "My food is to do the will of him who sent me, and to accomplish his work." Who will deny that this oneness of God and of His Christ *in function* is fundamental in a true preaching of Christ, and therefore also in the preaching of the whole counsel of God? In this sense the prophets preached Christ. He who was to come was seen to be in a unique sense the servant of God for man's salvation.

Some of the prophetic references to the mission of the Messiah bear a striking similarity to the actual ministry of Jesus Christ. We shall mention only a few, chiefly from the books of Isaiah and Jeremiah. Four of them have in common the unique prophetic word *Branch* (Hebrew *tsemach*). The first gives us a picture of the Christ as king (Jer. 23:5-6); the second pictures Him as a servant of God (Zech. 3:8), "my servant"); in the third we see Him as a man, "the man whose name is the Branch" (Zech. 6:12); the fourth is more enigmatic in character, but it may be a reference to "Messiah's beauty and glory" as a fruitbearing branch (Isa. 4:2). Fruitbearing is certainly implied in Isa. 11:1, where the Hebrew has another word for branch (netzer). Other passages reveal important qualities or aspects of His ministry. We note, for example the emphasis on justice, righteousness, and peace in Isa. 9; on righteousness, faithfulness, and peace in Isa. 11; on righteousness again in Jer. 33:15-16; on His appointment by God to be a mediator of "a (new) covenant to the people (of Israel)" and "a light to the nations" (Isa. 42:6-7); on the nature and purpose of His servant vocation in Isa. 49:5-7; on the suffering of the Lord's servant in Isa. 53, which reads almost like John's description and like Paul's interpretation of the Cross experience in the life of Jesus; on the mission of the Lord's anointed "to bring good tidings to the afflicted" (Isa. 61:1-3); on the shepherd who feeds his flock (Ezek. 34:23; Micah 5:4); on the triumphant and victorious reign which brings universal peace (Zech. 9:9-10). As we think through these more or less familiar portions of prophetic preaching we see the Christ in terms of His ministry as Savior and King: they preached Christ, and one purpose of their preaching was to create faith in God and in His promises of the coming of the Messiah to do His will and to accomplish His work.

But did they preach the crucifixion and the resurrection of Christ, His sufferings and the subsequent glory (I Peter 1:11)? Jesus himself said that they did. He can scarcely have meant that all of them did; nor that any one of them could testify of these things with the vividness of the historian who records an accomplished fact. There is a distinction always between prophecy and history, between foretelling and fulfilment; a distinction, if you will, between hope and faith in relation to the saving acts of God. The coming of Jesus Christ into the world, and His death and resurrection, gave concreteness and reality to the prophetic hope. Nevertheless the 53rd chapter of Isaiah is a truly remarkable description of the sufferings of the Man of Sorrows, and an equally remarkable interpretation of the spiritual significance of these sufferings, not only for Him who suffered but for us. There is no sufficient explanation of this chapter except as a direct prophecy of the sufferings of Christ. It is in a true sense the preaching of Christ Crucified, a testimony to the fact that the Savior must suffer for the sins of men in order to gain for them the victory over sin. The same truth is suggested, though not as systematically developed, in Zech. 12:10 and 13:1.

It is with regard to the resurrection of Christ that we find our greatest difficulty. What did Jesus mean when He said, "Thus it is written, that the Christ should suffer and on the third day rise from the dead"? Of what prophetic word was He thinking? How we wish that we had His full exegesis just at this point! But perhaps we do have a hint from Him in another connection, when speaking of the sign of Jonah. Jonah's life experience, which became a part of his preaching, testified as a type both of the death and of the resurrection of Christ. We do not mean to say that Jonah's generation so understood it. We would suggest with Ed. Böhl, however, that there is a sense in which the life experience of every believer from the time of the first gospel promise on (Gen. 3:15) bears the marks of suffering and glory, which prefigure not only the ongoing conflict between good and evil but also the final victory.[46] There may be even in the humiliation and exaltation of God's people, as seen in the Egyptian oppression and the Exodus redemption, or as represented by the

---

[46] Ed. Böhl, *Christologie des Alten Testaments,* p. 9 ff.

Babylonian Captivity experience, a typological foreshadowing of the truth that the way to victory lies through suffering. The spiritual victory note on which Isaiah 53 closes seems to be a testimony in the same direction. The constant emphasis on *the living God* in relation to His servant seems to presuppose this victory of life over death in the very person of the Messiah. Of course the preaching is not as clear as in the New Testament, but the fundamental principles involved are there. The case for the prophetic preaching of Christ's resurrection need not rest with Isaiah and Jonah: it roots in the very nature of the redemptive acts of God. The difference between then and now is that "we have the prophetic word made more sure" (II Peter 1:19), by the fulfilment of that word in the gospel; which also interprets its contents more precisely in terms of the new thing which God has done in fulfilling it.

C. *Concerning the Way of Salvation*

One thing is certain: the prophets preached the salvation of God, and they preached it in the same clear spiritual terms as the New Testament. We speak now of the Ordo Salutis, the Way of Salvation.

The two key words in this Way of Salvation as viewed from the angle of man's experience are repentance and faith. A third is the remission of sins, which is so closely related to, and in a sense contingent on, the first two.

Repentance! Both Jesus and Paul include it in their brief summaries of the whole counsel of God. It was the first word that Jesus preached. "Repent, for the kingdom of heaven is at hand" (Matt. 4:17). Paul preached it too, as we see especially from his Corinthian epistles. "I rejoice—because you were grieved into repenting;—for godly grief produces a repentance that leads to salvation and brings no regret" (see

II Cor. 7:9ff.). Repentance is necessary for salvation: not as a work of merit on the part of man, but as a humble seeking of the mercy of God. Without contrition and confession of sin God does not save men from sin. His salvation demands that we in heart and conscience repent of sin and turn from it to God, seeking from Him the power unto release from sin.

Did the prophets preach such a message of repentance? Indeed they did! Perhaps we should say that it was in this phase of preaching that they excelled. The note of repentance is a dominant note in their preaching.

They preached repentance in several ways. It may seem strange that they do not use the word "repent" in reference to men so much as in reference to an attitude of God. It is God who is represented as saying that He either will or will not repent. Repentance here means a change of attitude towards men according as they change theirs toward Him. Naturally, this is not repentance toward God or unto salvation. But whatever the terminology, the spiritual experience of repentance is definitely a goal of prophetic preaching.

We see this first from the many instances where they preach about sin. They run the whole gamut of individual and of social sins; and they indict it in a way which stings the conscience, and which cuts away every supporting prop that the sinner might suppose himself to have. We can only illustrate briefly here. Consider, for example, the six Woes of Isaiah 5. How vividly they indict the sin of landgrabbing, or insatiable greed (vs. 8-10); of dissipation, or drunken revelries (vs. 11-17); of blasphemous unbelief (vs. 18-19); of moral perversion (vs. 20); of self-conceit (vs. 21); of a misdirected heroism, which makes them excel in wine and wickedness (vs. 22-23)![47] Or consider Isaiah's preaching against the sin of drunkenness in high places:

---

[47] c.f. Geo. L. Robinson, *The International Standard Bible Encyclopedia*, 1925, art. "Isaiah."

These also reel with wine
  and stagger with strong drink;
the priest and the prophet reel with strong drink,
  they are confused with wine,
  they stagger with strong drink;
they err in vision,
  they stumble in giving judgment.
For all places are full of vomit,
  no place is without filthiness. (Isaiah 28:7-8)

Read the scathing strictures in Isaiah 59 (see especially verses 1-2, 5, 12-14); the dramatic characterization of Judah's guilt in Jeremiah 5:23-31 and 7:8-11, and in Ezekiel 16 (see verse 49) and 22; the Lord's controversy with His people in Hosea 4:1-2; the indictment of Israel in Amos 2:6-8 on a seven-fold count; the Woe against those who covet and oppress in Micah 2:1-2; the poignant statement in Hosea 2:13 that Israel "went after her lovers, and forgot me, says the Lord." These are just random selections. The sermons of the prophets abound in vivid pictures of sin, and of its consequences, which are designed to convict the sinner and to create sorrow of heart over sin and to cause him to return to God in sincere repentance.

They did more than paint word pictures of sin: they urged the sinful people to repent. They summoned them with words of invitation and of exhortation to repentance. No, they did not say it in just those words, as John and Jesus did, "Repent ye!" They did use the Hebrew verb *shuv*, which means *turn;* it is translated *repent* in Ezekiel 18:30 (RSV). But they did something else that brings out the idea of repentance just as clearly and strongly and searchingly as if they had used the imperative, "Repent!" Who is not familiar with the pleading call in Isaiah 55:6-9:

Seek the Lord while he may be found,
  call upon him while he is near;

> *let the righteous forsake his way,*
>   *and the unrighteous man his thoughts;*
> *let him return to the Lord, that he may have mercy on him,*
>   *and to our God, for he will abundantly pardon.*
> *For my thoughts are not your thoughts,*
>   *neither are your ways my ways, says the Lord.*
> *For as the heavens are higher than the earth,*
>   *so are my ways higher than your ways*
>   *and my thoughts than your thoughts.*

We are reminded of Paul's question in Romans 2:4, "Do you not know that God's kindness is meant to lead you to repentance?" The prophets knew it. Whether they preached the wrath of God or the love of God they sought thereby to lead their people to repentance. "You will seek me and find me; when you seek me with all your heart, I will be found by you, says the Lord" (Jer. 29:13-14).

> *Seek the Lord and live,*
>   *lest he break out like fire in the house of Joseph,*
>   *and it devour, with none to quench it for Bethel,*
> *O you who turn justice to wormwood,*
>   *and cast down righteousness to the earth!* (Amos 5:6)

> *Seek good, and not evil,*
>   *that you may live;*
> *and so the Lord, the God of hosts, will be with you,*
>   *as you have said.*
> *Hate evil, and love good,*
>   *and establish justice in the gate;*
> *it may be that the Lord, the God of hosts,*
>   *will be gracious to the remnant of Joseph.* (Amos 5:14-15)

> *Return to the Lord your God,*
>   *for he is gracious and merciful,*
> *slow to anger, and abounding in steadfast love,*
>   *and repents of evil.* (Joel 2:13)

"Say to them, As I live, says the Lord God, I have no pleasure in the death of the wicked, but that the wicked turn from his way and live; turn back, turn back from your evil ways; for why will you die, O house of Israel?" (Ezek. 33:11; see also Ezek. 18:23, 30-32 and Hos. 12:6). Underlying these and scores of other passages is the plea of the preacher in the name of the Lord, "Turn! Turn away from sin! Turn back to God!" That means to repent. Seek the Lord earnestly and sincerely, and He will be found; for He has no pleasure in the death of sinners: it is His will that they should turn and live. But the soul that persists in sinning shall die. There can be no peace, says God, for the wicked. (See Isa. 57:21.)

I for one am frankly of the opinion that we could learn something from the prophets in the way of bold and effective preaching of repentance. We could learn this that they did not mince words in calling sin by its right name; but also this that they did not denounce sin as if such denunciation were an end in itself. Sin and grace are set side by side in their preaching. They aim to put the fear of God into the heart; but all the time there are undertones, or overtones, as you prefer, of tenderly pleading divine love. The repentance of the sinner is toward God; and God is a Savior, whose own seeking of the sinner gives him grace to turn and to trust.

For faith in God as Savior, Redeemer, and Lord is the goal of prophetic preaching. If there is faith there will be new life. If there is faith there can be a new experience of divine fellowship and blessing. If there is faith there can be forgiveness, and righteousness, and peace. If there is faith there can be a restoration and a renewal and even a transformation of the covenant relationship between God and His people. Even as love on the part of God, so faith on the part of man is fundamental to any true covenant between the two; and this the prophets understood and preached almost as clearly as we. They did not use the word faith as often as we do; but they sought it nevertheless in their preaching. A trusting faith in the God of steadfast love; an obedient faith in response to the covenant grace of God; a faith which is assured of the forgiveness of sins because it relies on God who is "merciful and gracious, slow to anger, and abounding in steadfast love and faithfulness, keeping steadfast love for thousands, forgiving iniquity and transgression and sin" (Exod. 34:6, 7): a faith which in a true sense may be said to be "in our Lord Jesus Christ," because the love which sent Christ and the love which we see in Christ is none other than the love of God. (See John 3:16; Rom. 8:37-39.) It is true that the prophets did not see Christ as we do, nor could they speak of His love as we can. The past tense of Galatians 2:20, "who loved me and gave himself for me," could not be used until after the historical event of Calvary; but the love of God did not begin there. The saving acts of God began in the moment when man first sinned; and from that moment on the redemptive love of God is evident to the eye of faith. The prophets believed in the salvation of God. Sometimes they spoke of it as the coming of God Himself to redeem His people and to be their Savior. Sometimes they seemed to connect this redemption with one whom God would send to be His servant in this work of saving love. Does it really matter so much whether they looked to God for salvation or to the servant whom He purposed to send in the fulness of time? They saw the Savior; and as they sought Him, they received in their hearts the same assurance of pardon and peace and power as we receive through faith in Jesus. For did He not say, "I and the Father are one"? (John 10:30). If it be true that he who has seen Jesus has seen the Father (John 14:9) the reverse must also be true, that in every saving act of the living God since the creation of the world there is revealed something of the divine love so completely expressed in Christ and in His Cross. We cannot pursue the thought further now, but it is worth thinking through. For the moment we turn to a few of the many prophetic passages that reveal something of this love of God which is the guarantee of mercy and forgiveness beyond merit or measure, and which therefore becomes in the Old Testament as well as in the New the foundation of faith.

We have already quoted Isa. 55:6-7 in connection with repentance. It is worth quoting again in connection with faith.

> *Seek the Lord while he may be found,*
>   *call upon him while he is near;*
> *let the wicked forsake his way,*
>   *and the unrighteous man his thoughts;*
> *let him return to the Lord, that he may have mercy on him,*
>   *and to our God, for he will abundantly pardon.*

This is pure gospel, and a sure foundation for the penitent sinner's faith!

So also is the message of God's steadfast love in the book of Hosea. Jesus seems to have loved the keynote sentence in this book, "For I desire steadfast love (or mercy) and not sacrifice" (6:6); see his use of it in connection with his own ministry in Matthew 9:13 and 12:7. Hosea 11:8-9 is a wonderful commentary on this same text:

> *How can I give you up, O Ephraim!*
>   *How can I hand you over, O Israel!*
> *How can I make you like Admah!*
>   *How can I treat you like Zeboiim!*
> *My heart recoils within me,*
>   *my compassion grows warm and tender.*
> *I will not execute my fierce anger,*
>   *I will not again destroy Ephraim;*
> *for I am God and not man,*
>   *the Holy One in your midst,*
>   *and I will not come to destroy.*

This too is the good news of God's love; the same love which found its supreme expression when He sent His Son into the world, "not to condemn the world, but that the world might be saved through him" (see John 3:16-17). The point that we would make is this: when the prophets preached the love of God it was not something other than but an anticipation of "the love of God in Christ Jesus our Lord" (Rom. 8:39). Such preaching lays a sure foundation for faith.

A few additional examples of the same kind of preaching may be given without comment.

> *Thou dost keep him in perfect peace,*
>   *whose mind is stayed on thee,*
>   *because he trusts in thee.* (Isaiah 26:3)

> *Surely he has borne our griefs*
>   *and carried our sorrows;*
> *yet we esteemed him stricken,*
>   *smitten by God, and afflicted.*
> *But he was wounded for our transgressions,*
>   *he was bruised for our iniquities;*
> *upon him was the chastisement that made us whole,*
>   *and with his stripes we are healed.*
> *All we like sheep have gone astray;*
>   *we have turned every one to his own way;*
> *and the Lord has laid on him*
>   *the iniquity of us all.* (Isaiah 53:4-6)

> *For thus says the high and lofty One*
>   *who inhabits eternity, whose name is Holy:*
> *"I dwell in the high and holy place,*
>   *and also with him who is of a contrite and humble spirit,*
> *to revive the spirit of the humble,*
>   *and to revive the heart of the contrite.*
> *For I will not contend for ever,*
>   *nor will I always be angry;*
> *for from me proceeds the spirit,*
>   *and I have made the breath of life."* (Isaiah 57:15-16)

> *I have loved you with an everlasting love;*
>   *therefore I have continued my faithfulness to you.*
>   (Jeremiah 31:3)

In all their affliction he was afflicted,
  and the angel of his presence saved them;
in his love and in his pity he redeemed them;
  he lifted them up and carried them all the days of old.
                                    (Isaiah 63:9)

I will heal their faithlessness;
  I will love them freely,
  for my anger has turned from them. (Hosea 14:4)

I will speak to her heart (see Hebrew of Hosea 2:14c)

He will rejoice over you with gladness,
  he will renew you in [ASV, *rest in*] *his love.*
                                    (Zephaniah 3:17)

We could continue almost indefinitely; for the illustrations go beyond what we may call "proof passages" or "quotable quotes": they include the very fabric of the prophetic concept of the covenant God and Redeemer in relation to His people and to His purpose for the world.

Conclusion

What we have sought to do is to deepen the conviction that there is a fundamental unity in the Scriptures: the covenant of blessing with Abraham is the vehicle for a gospel preached beforehand; a foundation of divine grace underlies the Mosaic covenant at Sinai as well as the Calvary covenant in the blood of Christ; the prophets as well as the apostles preached a message which can rightly be called "The whole counsel of God": a message about God the Savior, about redemption in a profoundly religious sense, about God's Messiah and Servant who would accomplish His work, about the way of salvation as originating in the grace of God, about repentance and faith, about the forgiveness of sins as the choicest spiritual gift of God's love. Men were saved by grace through faith in the days of Isaiah, as they had been in the days of Abraham; for wherever the living God, who is the only Savior, seeks sinners, and they repent and believe, it is sufficient for salvation. There has never been more than one Savior, and that is God; for "God was in Christ reconciling the world to himself" (II Cor. 5:19). There has never been more than one way of salvation, the way of repentance to God and faith in the promises of God which reach their climax and fulfilment in Jesus Christ; for "Through him you have confidence in God, who raised him from the dead and gave him glory, so that your faith and hope are in God" (I Peter 1:21). The saving acts of God revealed in the Old Testament are one in spirit and purpose with the saving work of Christ in the New. The love of God as experienced by His people Israel is none other than the love that we see in deepest measure in Jesus Christ. While the prophets did not have the fulness of the gospel in the sense in which it was actualized in Christ they were preachers of the one God, the one Savior, the one way of salvation by grace through repentance and faith: and therefore, in the final analysis, of Christ and of "the whole counsel of God."

Bibliography

Riehm, Ed.: *Messianic Prophecy.*

Hebert, A. G.: *The Throne of David.*

Jacob, Edmond: *Theology of the Old Testament.*

Moffatt, James: *A New Translation of the Bible.*

McFadyen, J. E.: *A Cry for Justice.*

Milton, J. P.: *God's Word to Men.*

Bracker, D.: *Der Knecht Jehova.*

Davis, John D.: *A Dictionary of the Bible.*

Davidson, A. B.: *The Theology of the Old Testament.*

Smith-Goodspeed: *The Bible: An American Translation.*

Weymouth, Richard Francis: *The New Testament in Modern Speech.*

American Jewish Version of the Old Testament.

The Christian Century, March 6, 1957.

Christianity Today, December 24, 1956.

Sellin, Ernst: *Das A. T. im christlichen Gottesdienst und Unterricht.*

Möller, Wilhelm: *Inledning till Gamla Testamentet* (Swedish translation from the German).

Luther, Martin: *Small Catechism.*

The Westminster Dictionary of the Bible.

Girdlestone, R. B.: *The Synonyms of the Old Testament.*

Vos, Geerhardus: *Biblical Theology.*

Whitehouse, W. A., in Richardson's *A Theological Word Book of the Bible,* article *Law.*

Milton, J. P.: *The Psalms.*

Böhl, Ed.: *Christologie des Alten Testaments.*

Swedish Version of the Bible, 1917.

American Standard Version of the Bible.

Revised Standard Version of the Bible.

The Hebrew Bible.

Smith, George Adam: *The Book of Isaiah,* in the *Expositor's Bible.*

Robinson, Geo. L.: in *International Standard Bible Encyclopedia,* article *Isaiah.*